The Legendary
Scribble-Scrabble Book

for your
Tattoos

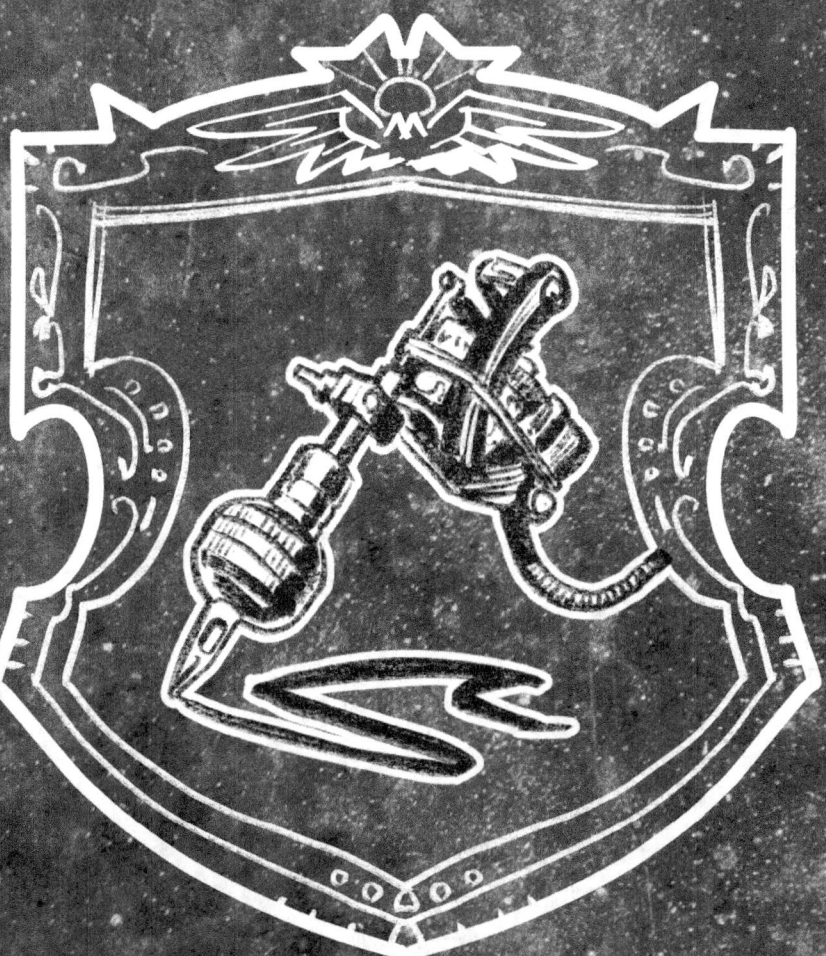

Ute Wuensch-Cloerkes

»The Legendary Scribble-Scrabble Book for Your Tattoos«
© 2019 Wuensch, First Edition

Based on: Wuensch: »Das legendaere Krakel-Kritzel-Buch fuer deine Tattoos«,
published 2019 by BoD, Norderstedt, Germany

Author: Ute Wuensch-Cloerkes
www.uuu-online.de
Illustrator: Oliver Wuensch
www.wuenschonline.de
Graphik: Ute Wuensch-Cloerkes

Published and printed by: KDP Kindle Direct Publishing
Amazon Europe Core SARL, Société à responsabilité limitée,
38 avenue John F. Kennedy, L-1855 Luxemburg

ISBN: 978-1-7024-6621-9
Imprint: Independently published

Design your

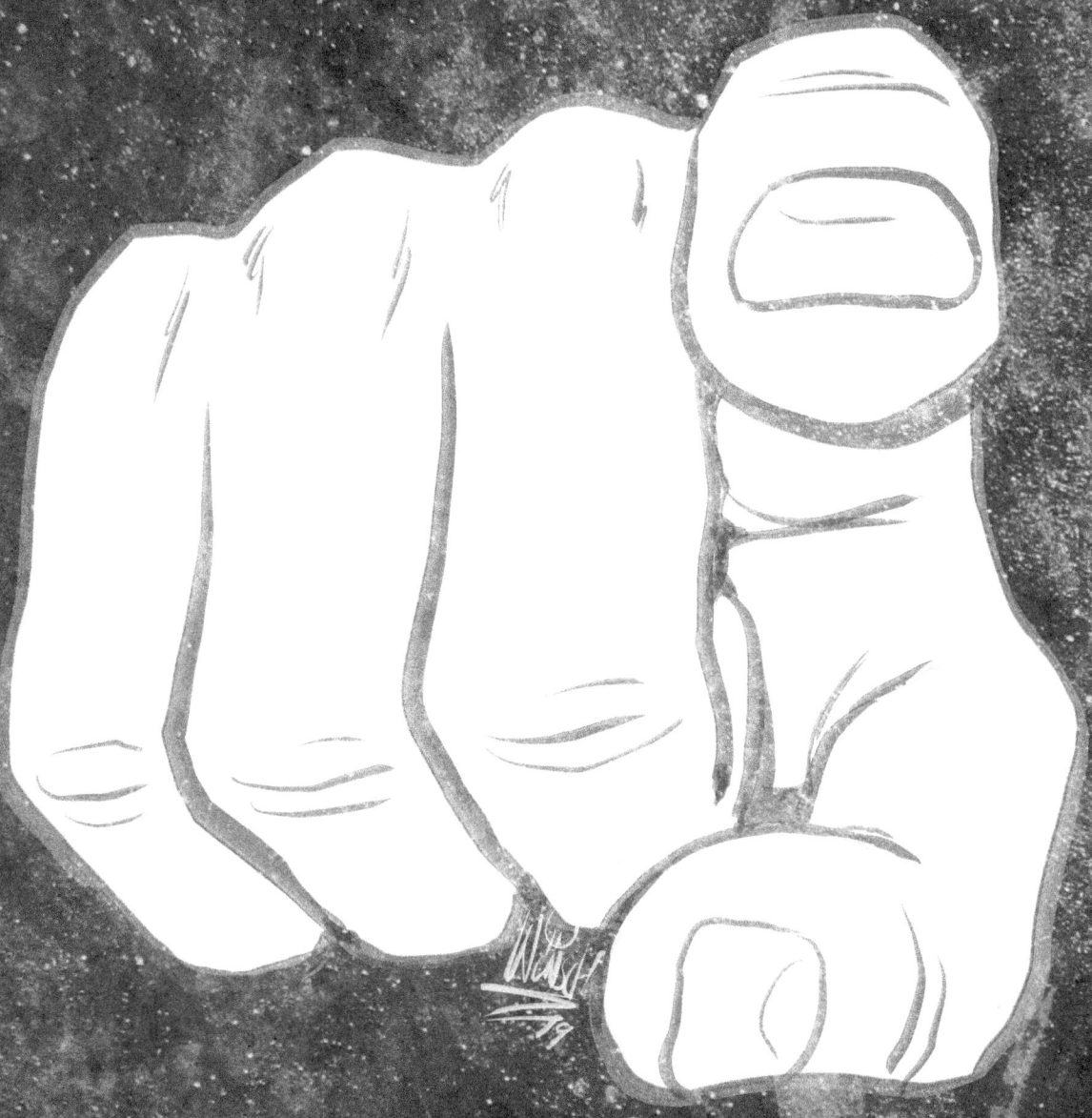

own Tattoo!

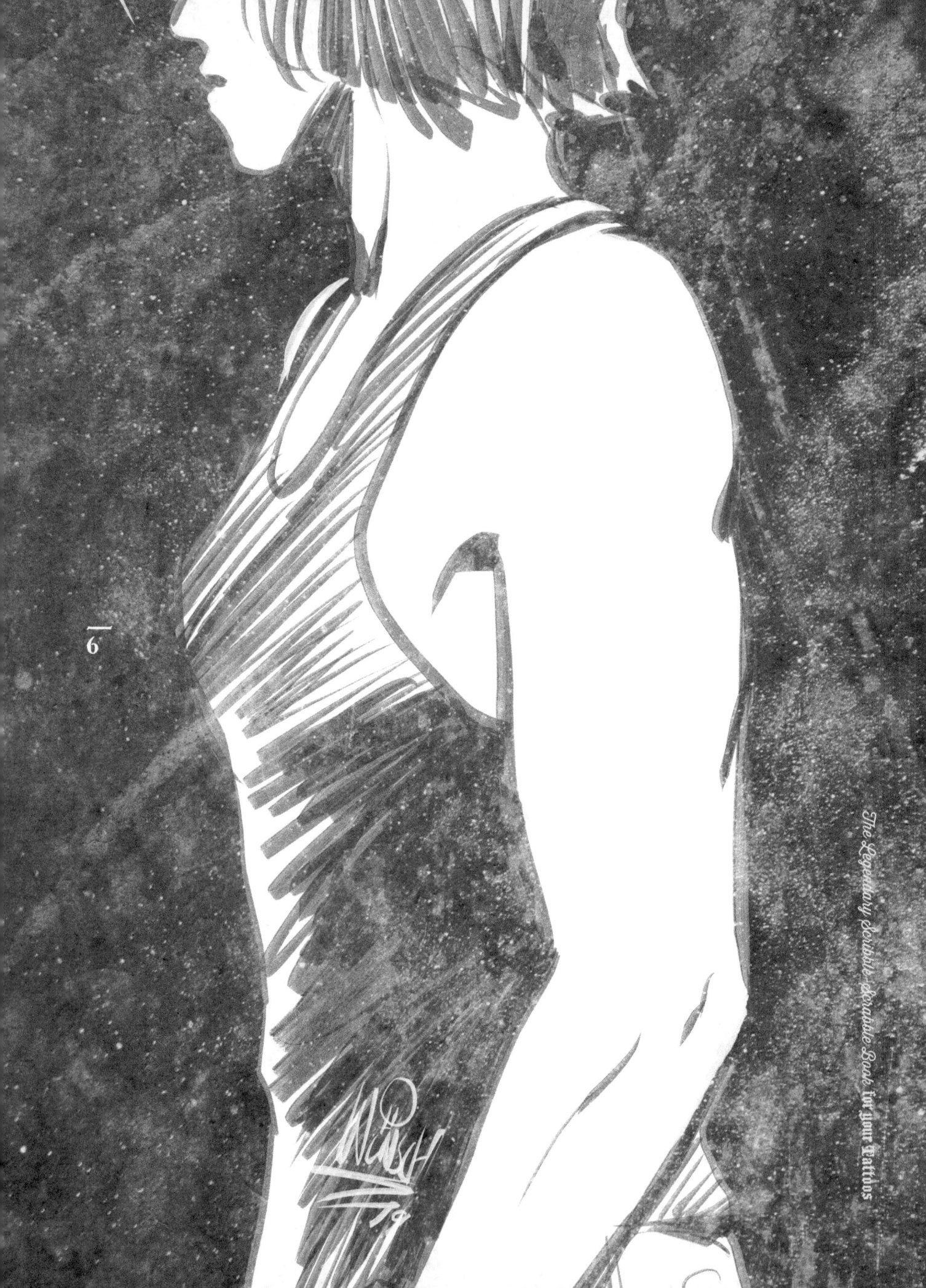

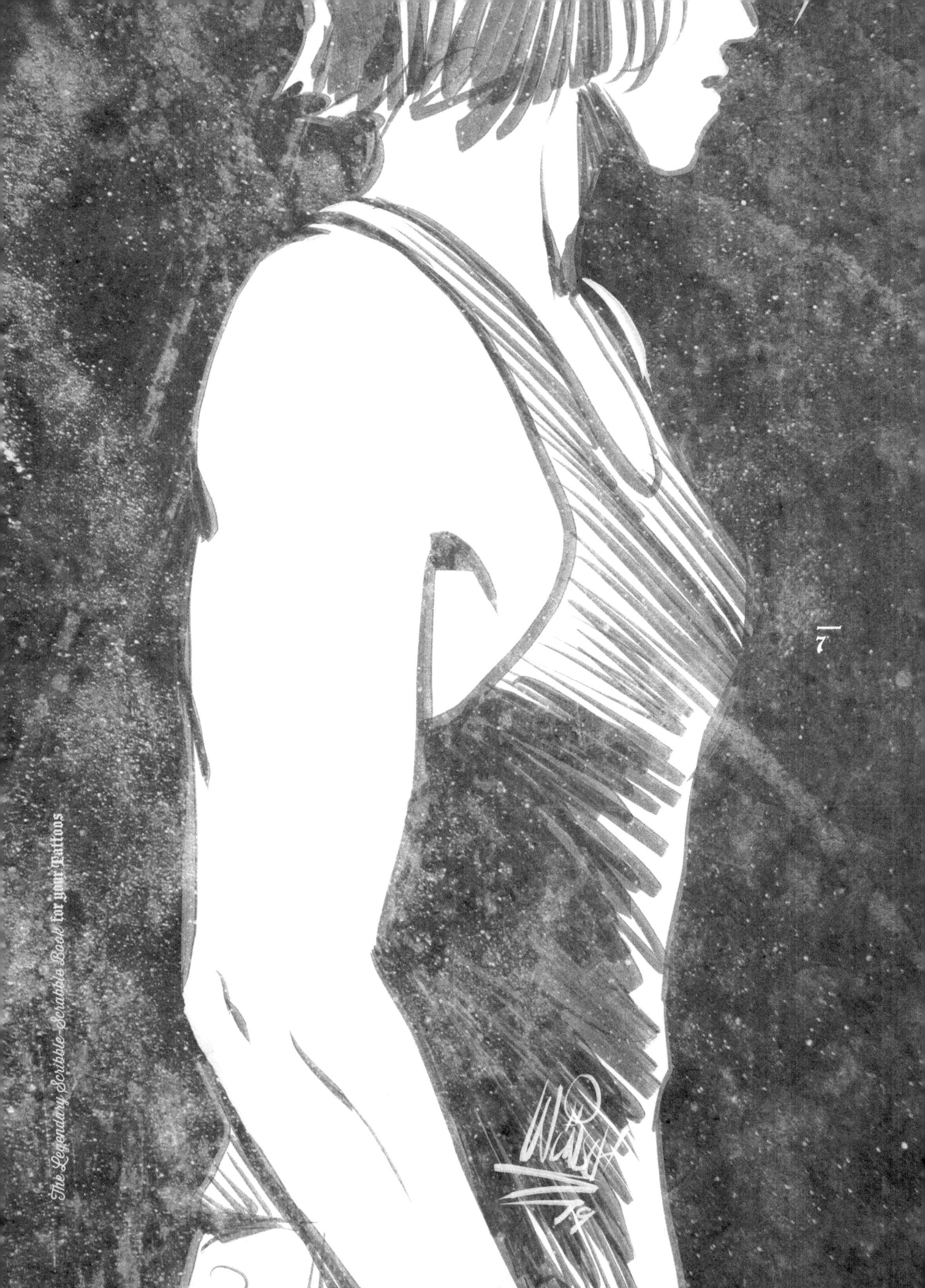

7

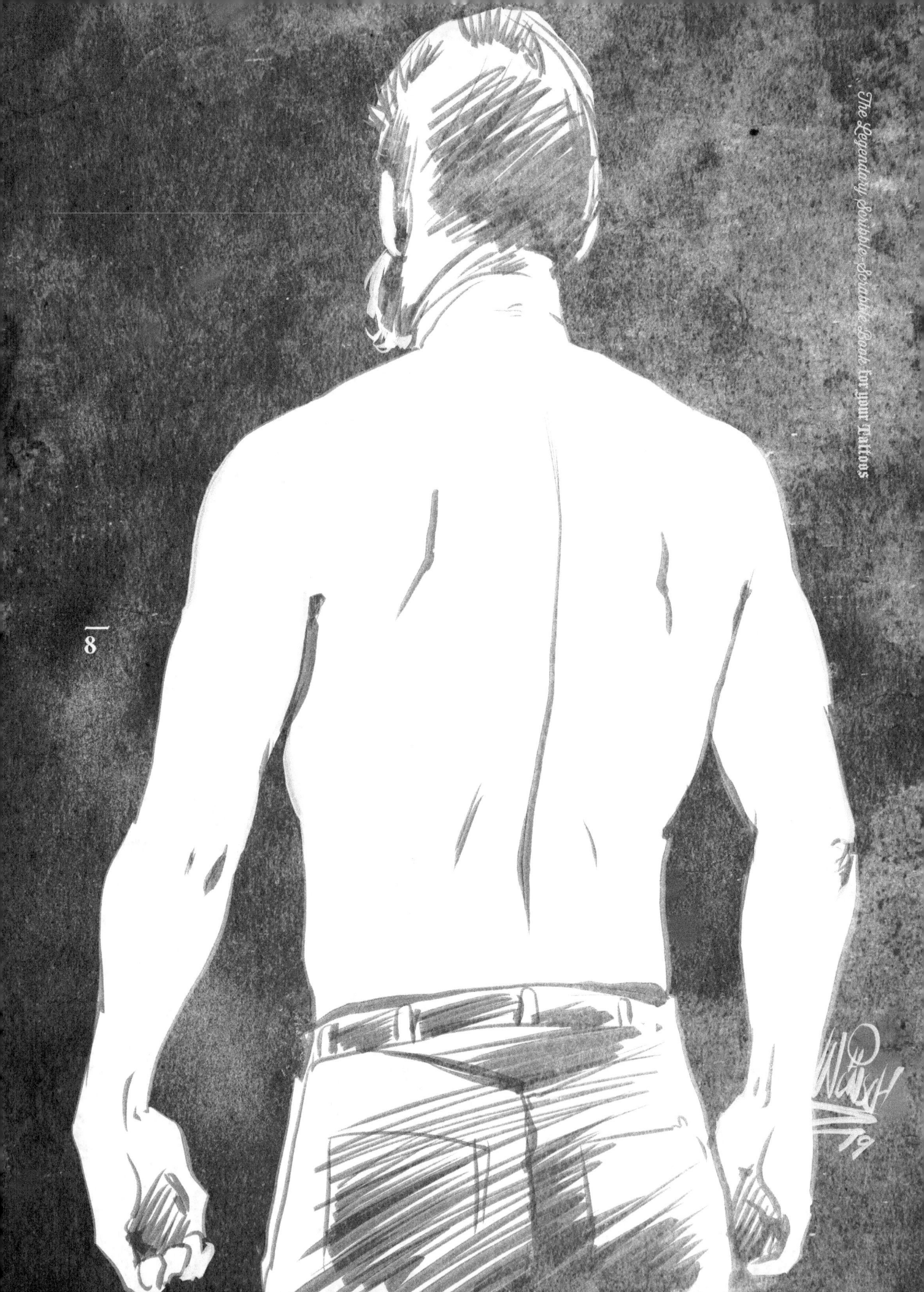

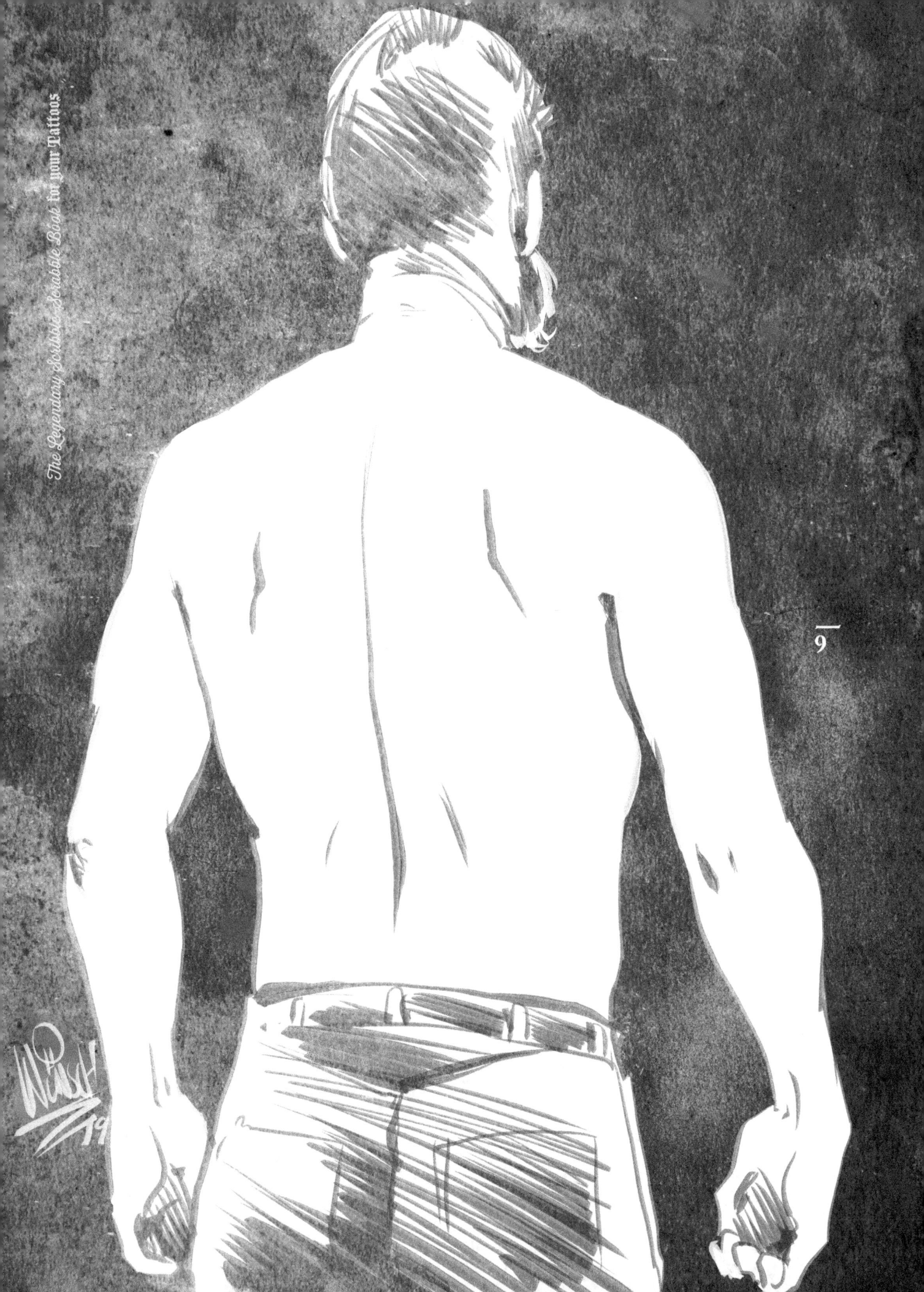

9

10

11

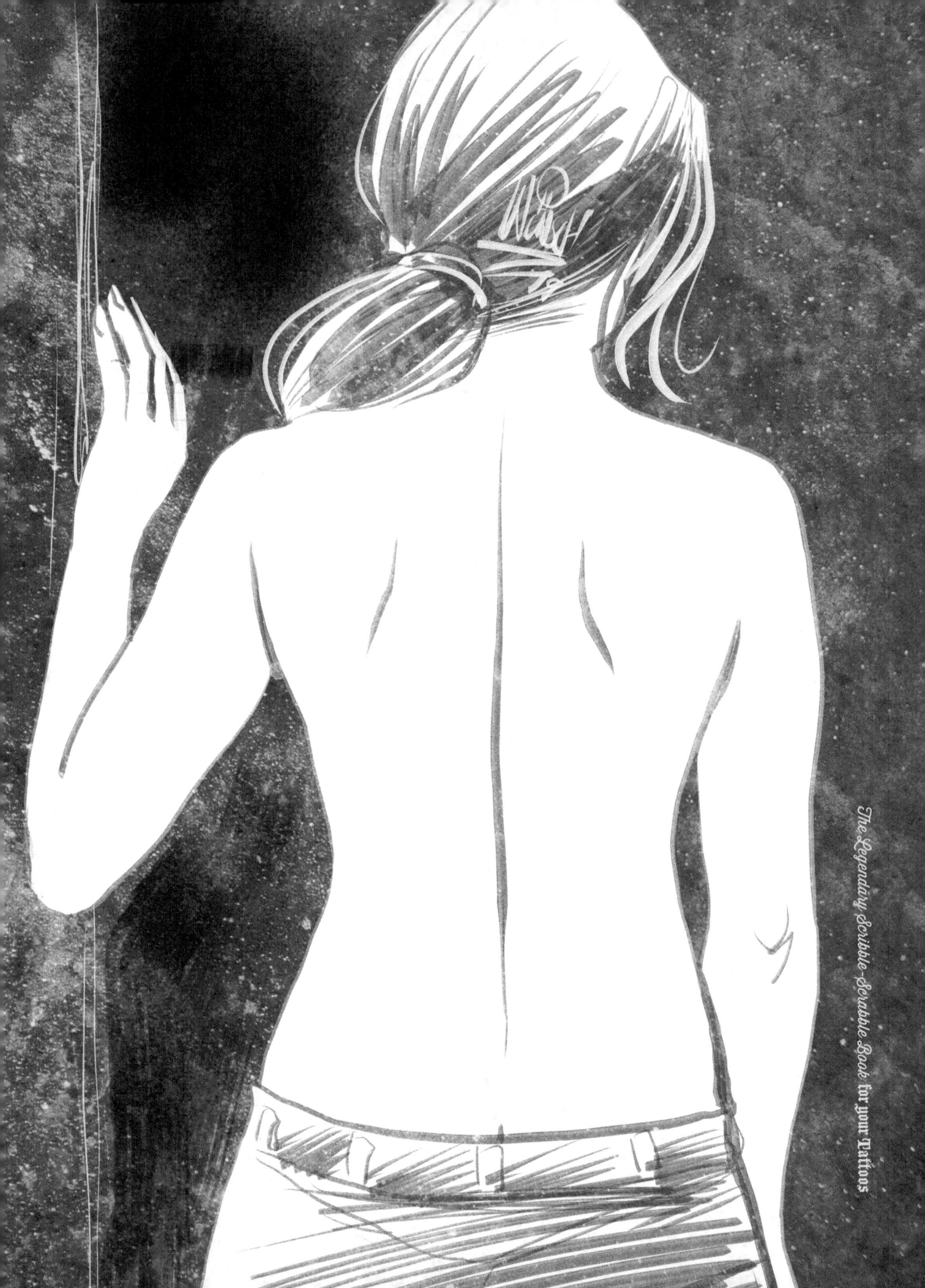

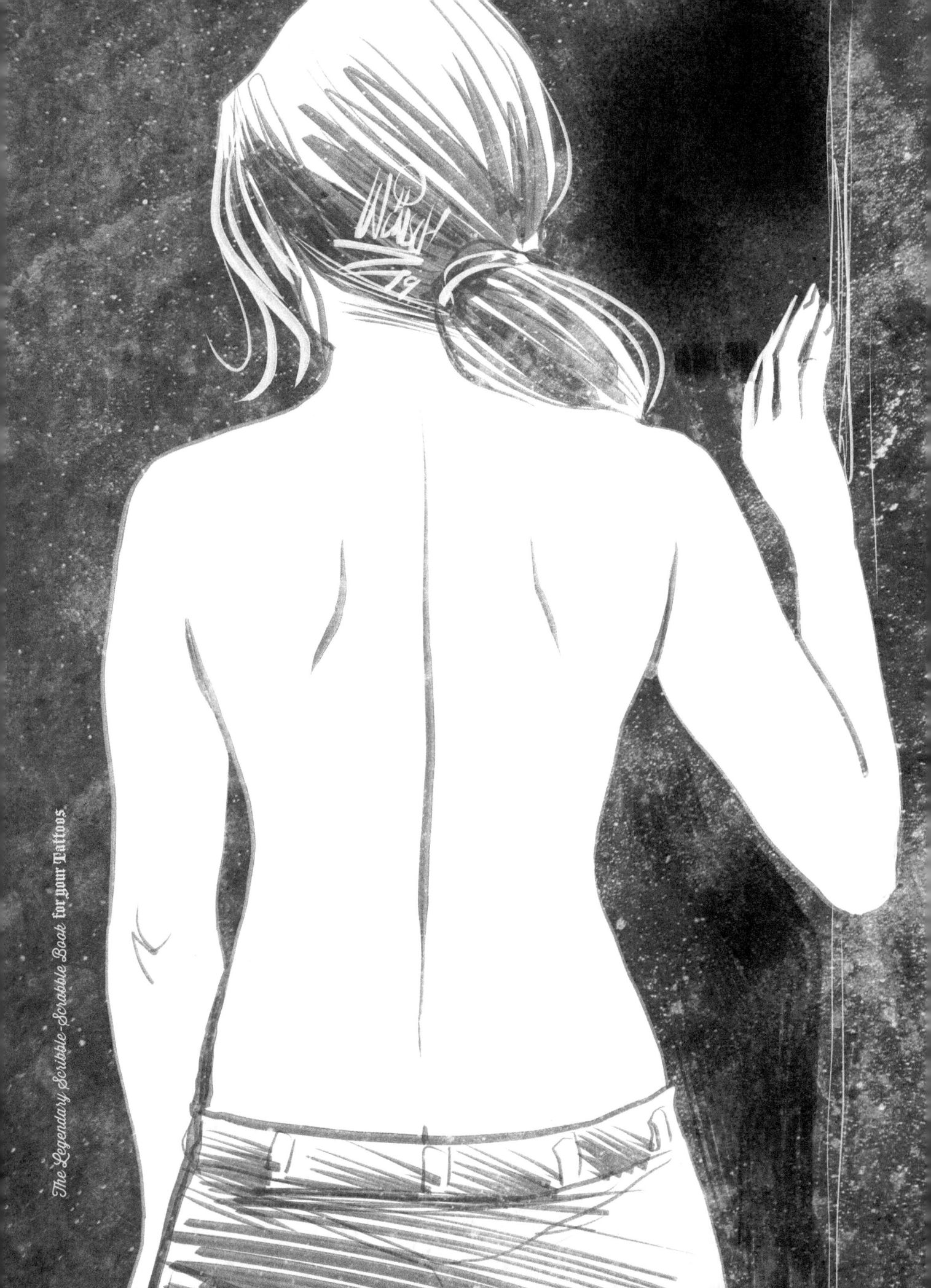

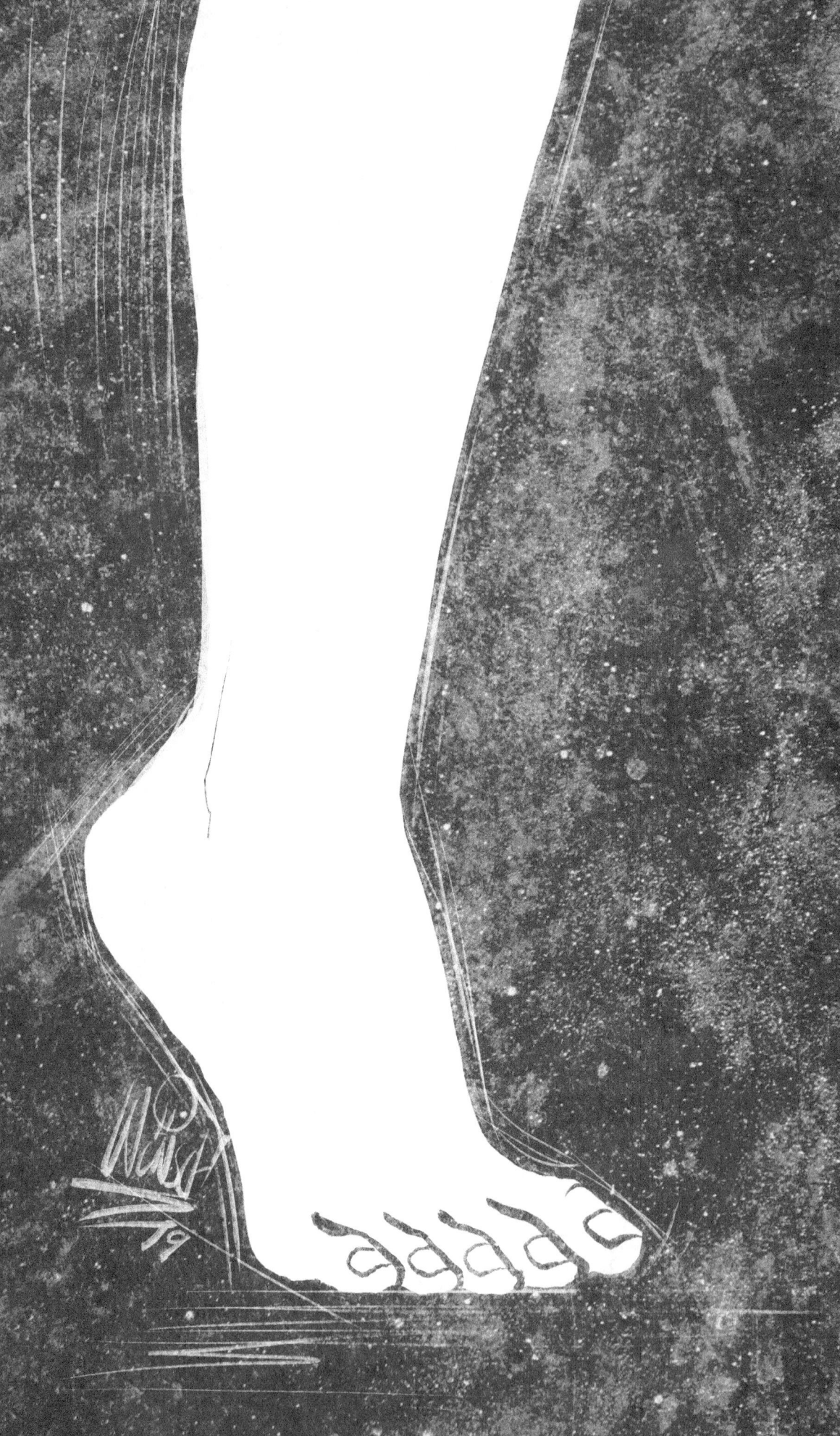

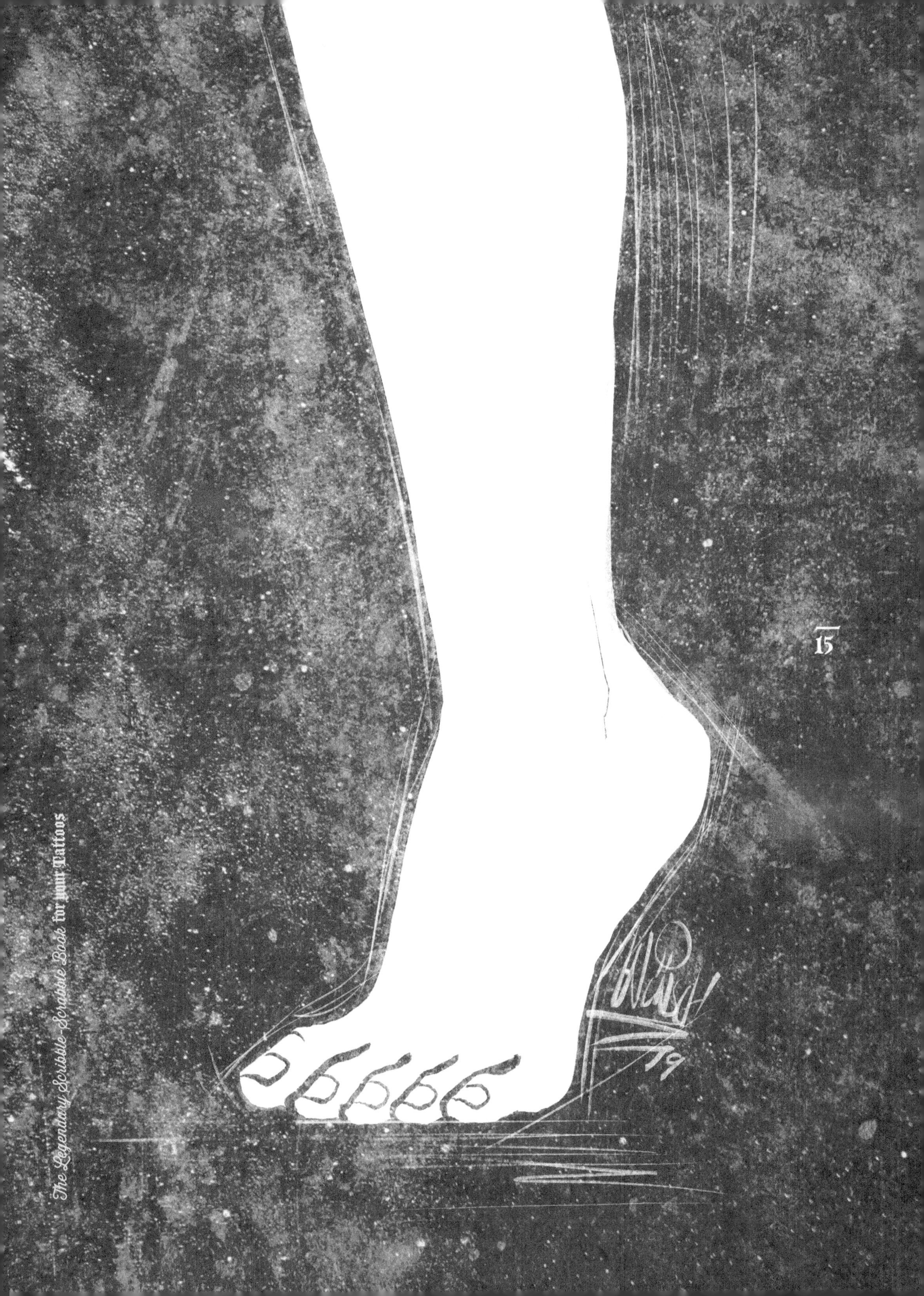

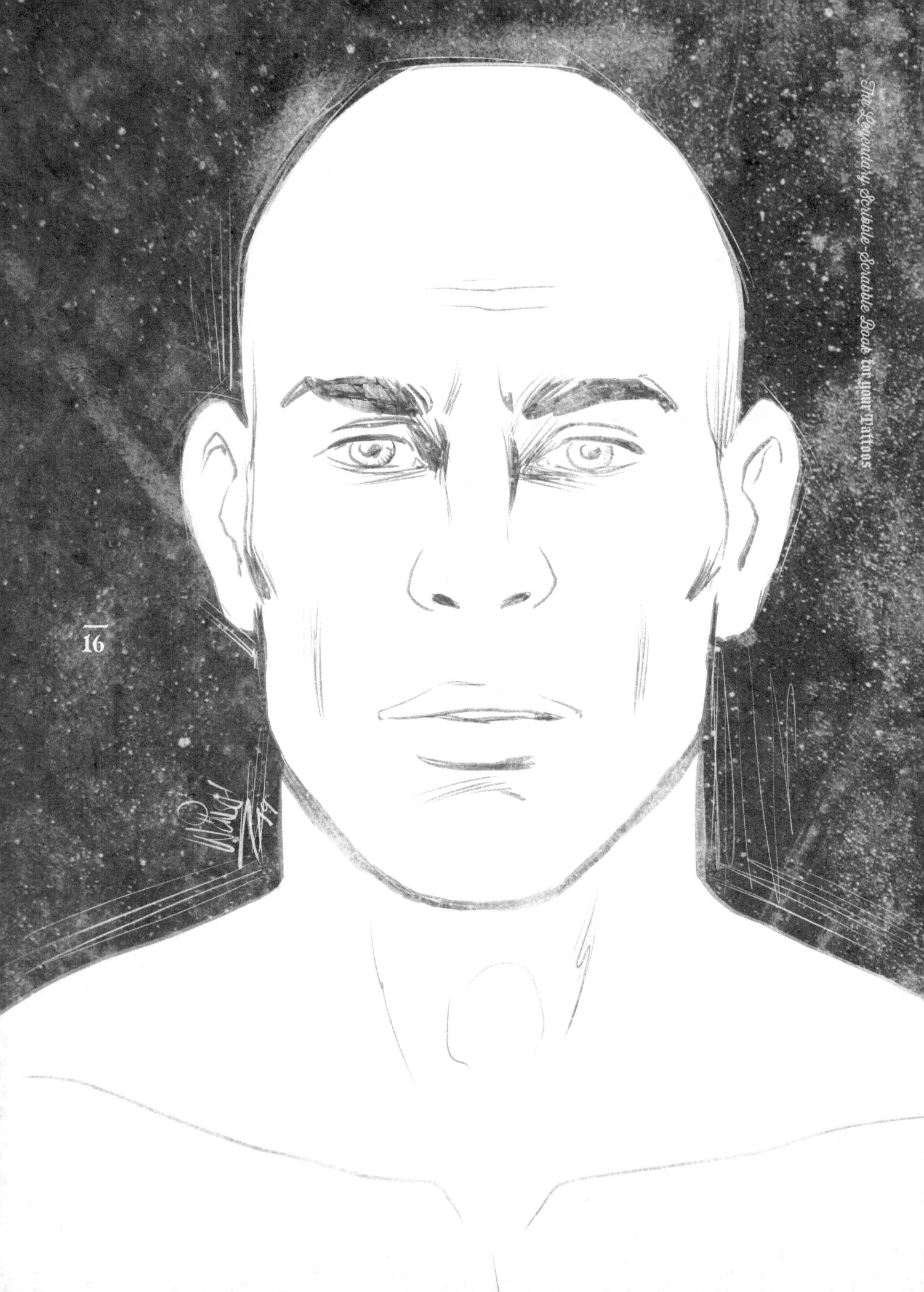

16

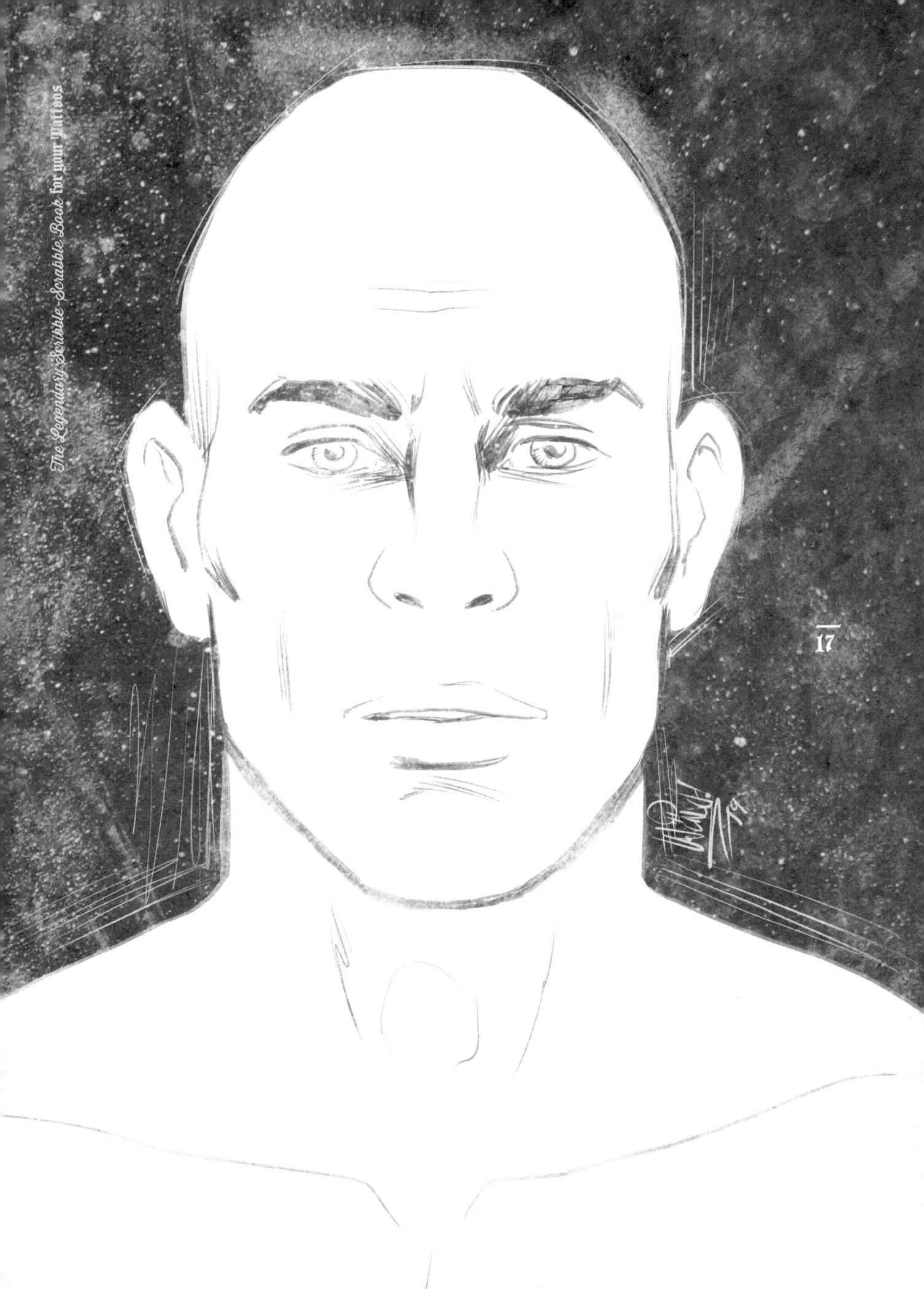

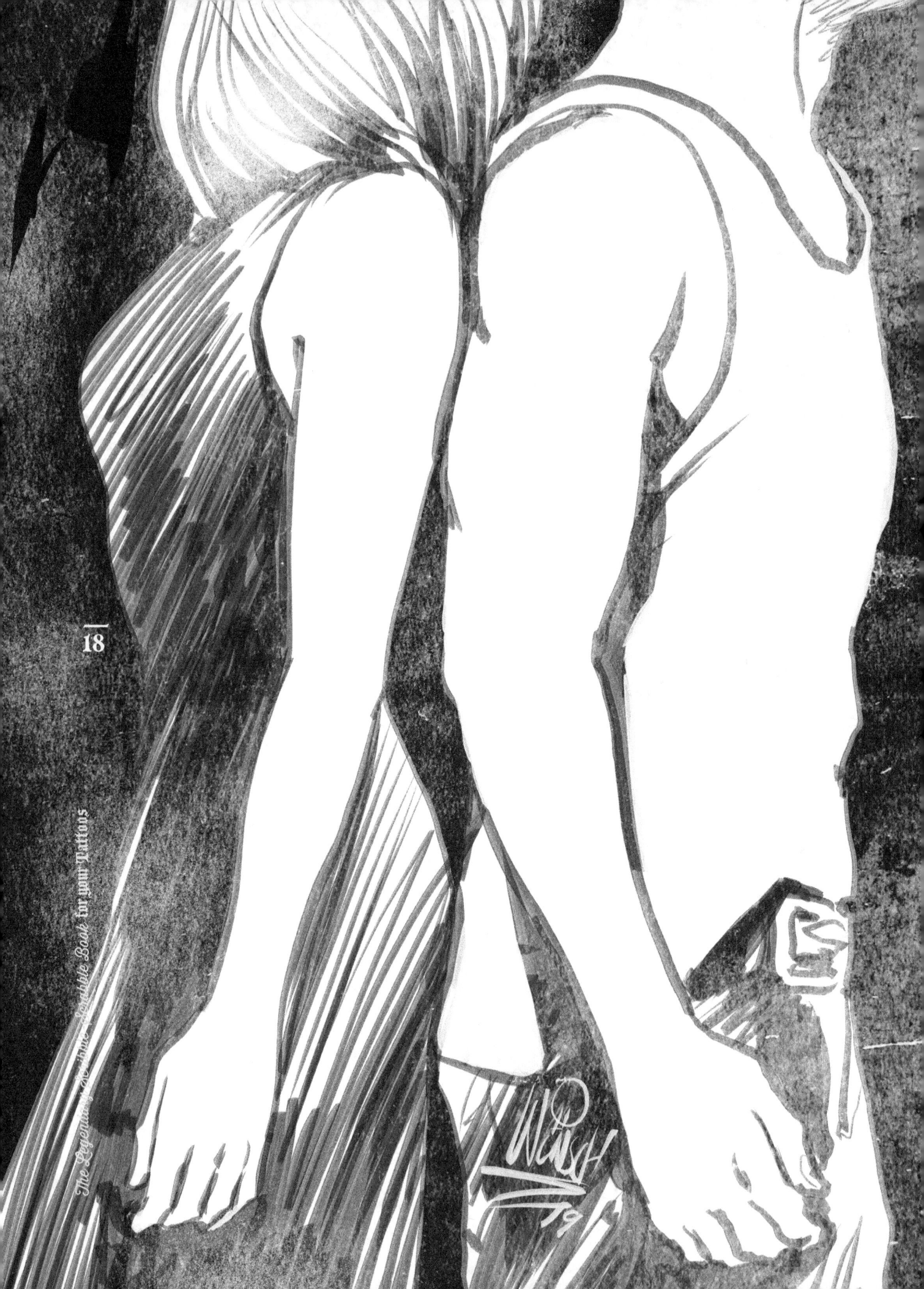

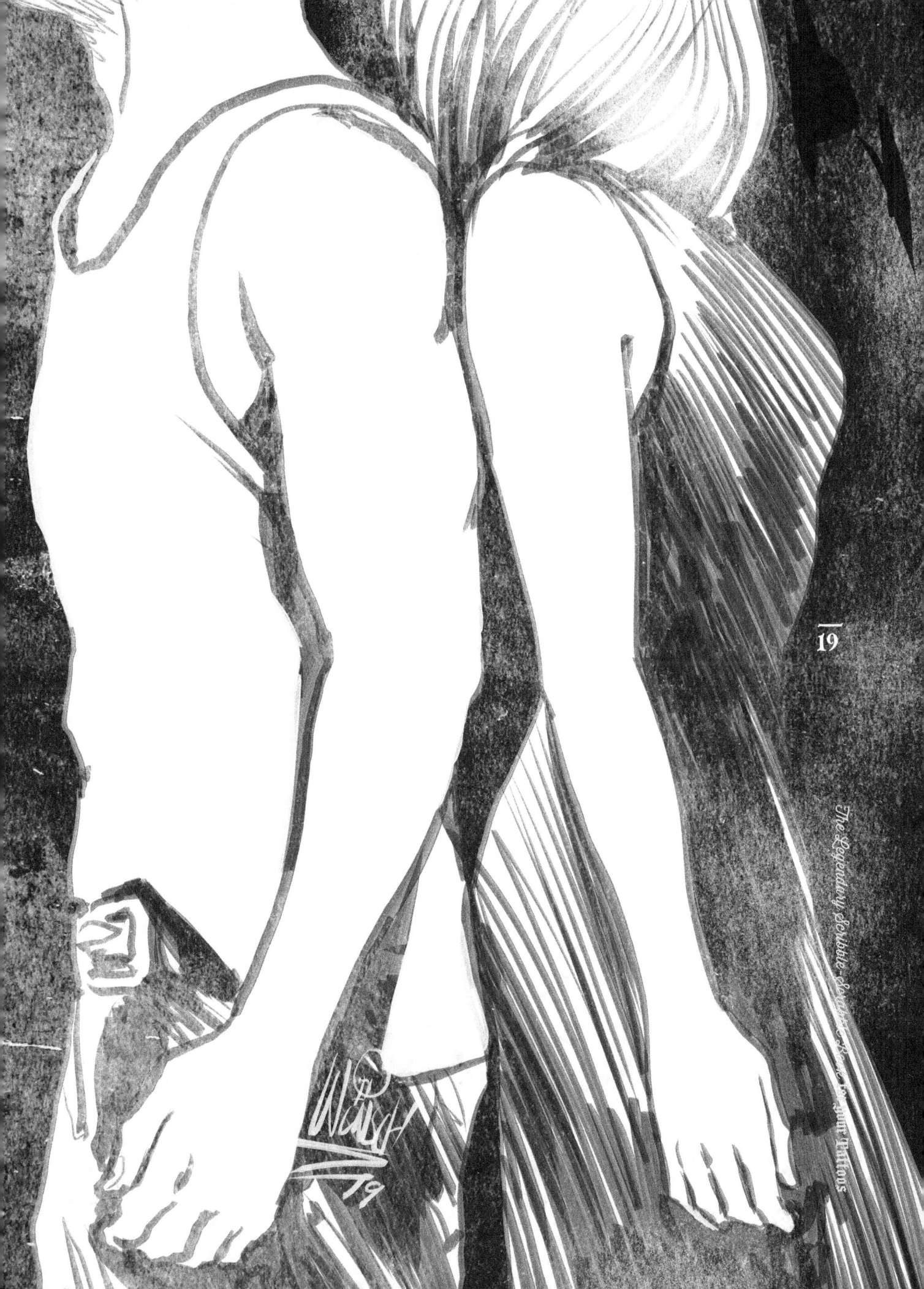

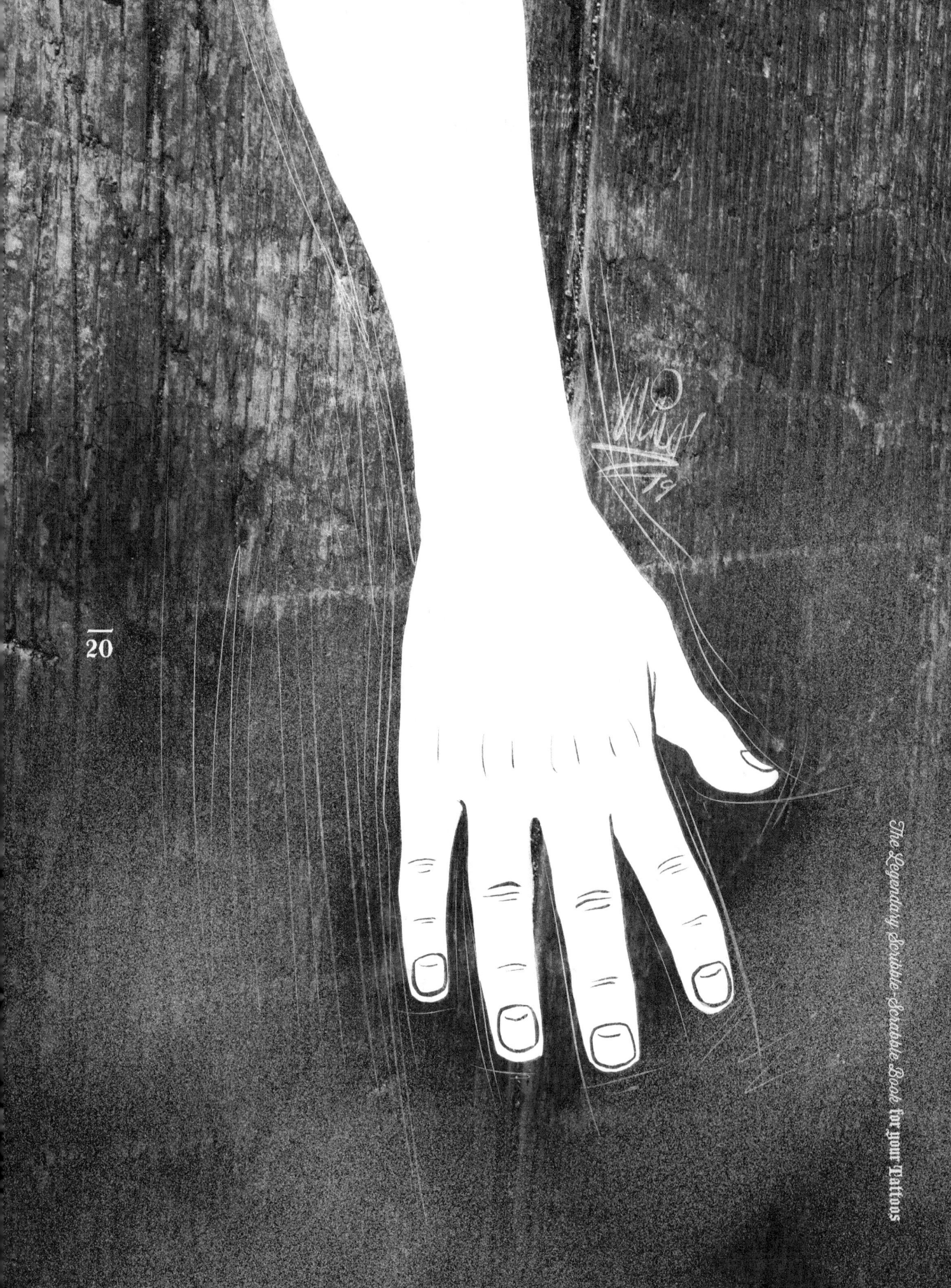

The Legendary Scribble-Scrabble-Book for your Tattoos

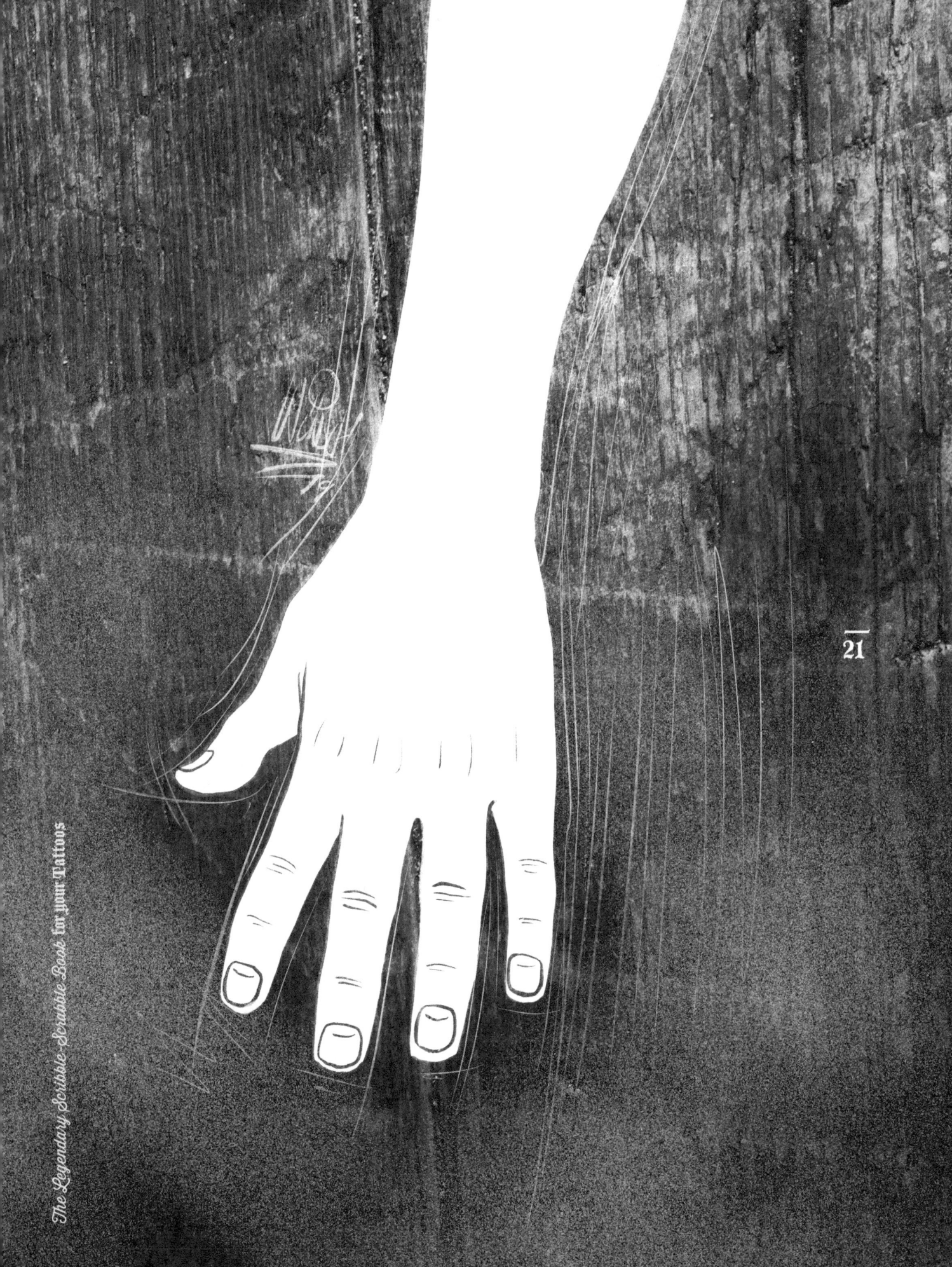

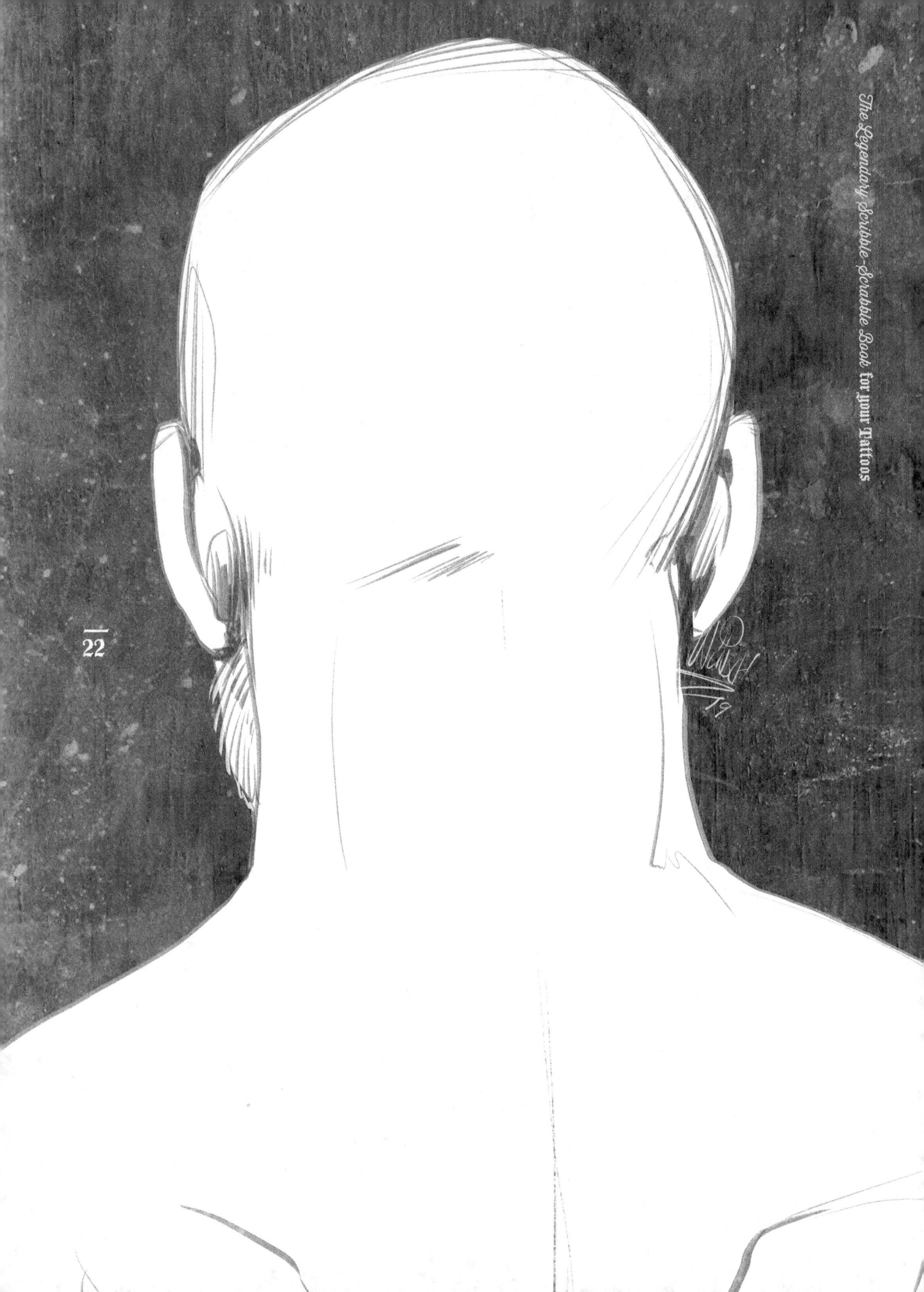

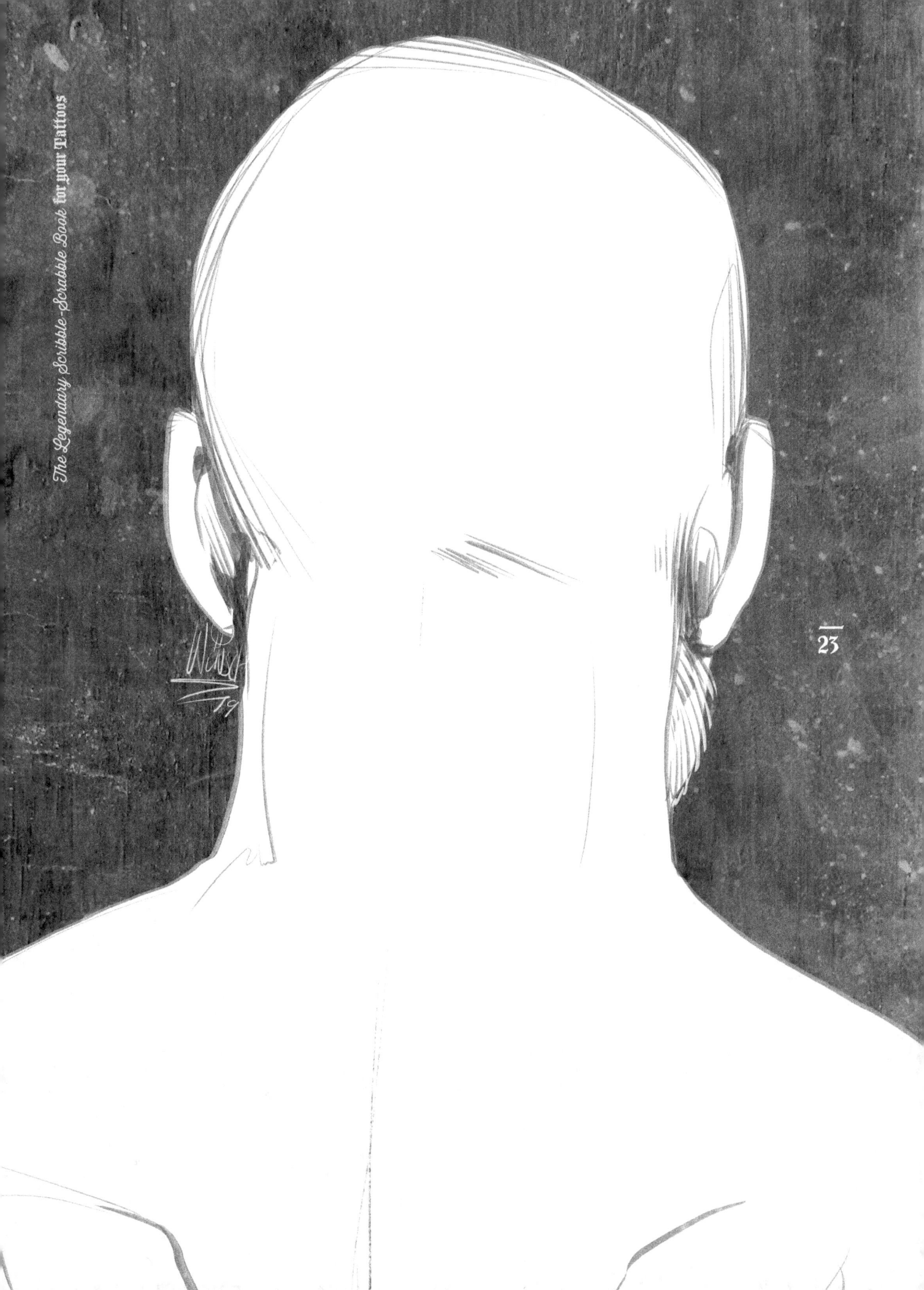

The Legendary Scribble-Scrabble Book for your Tattoos

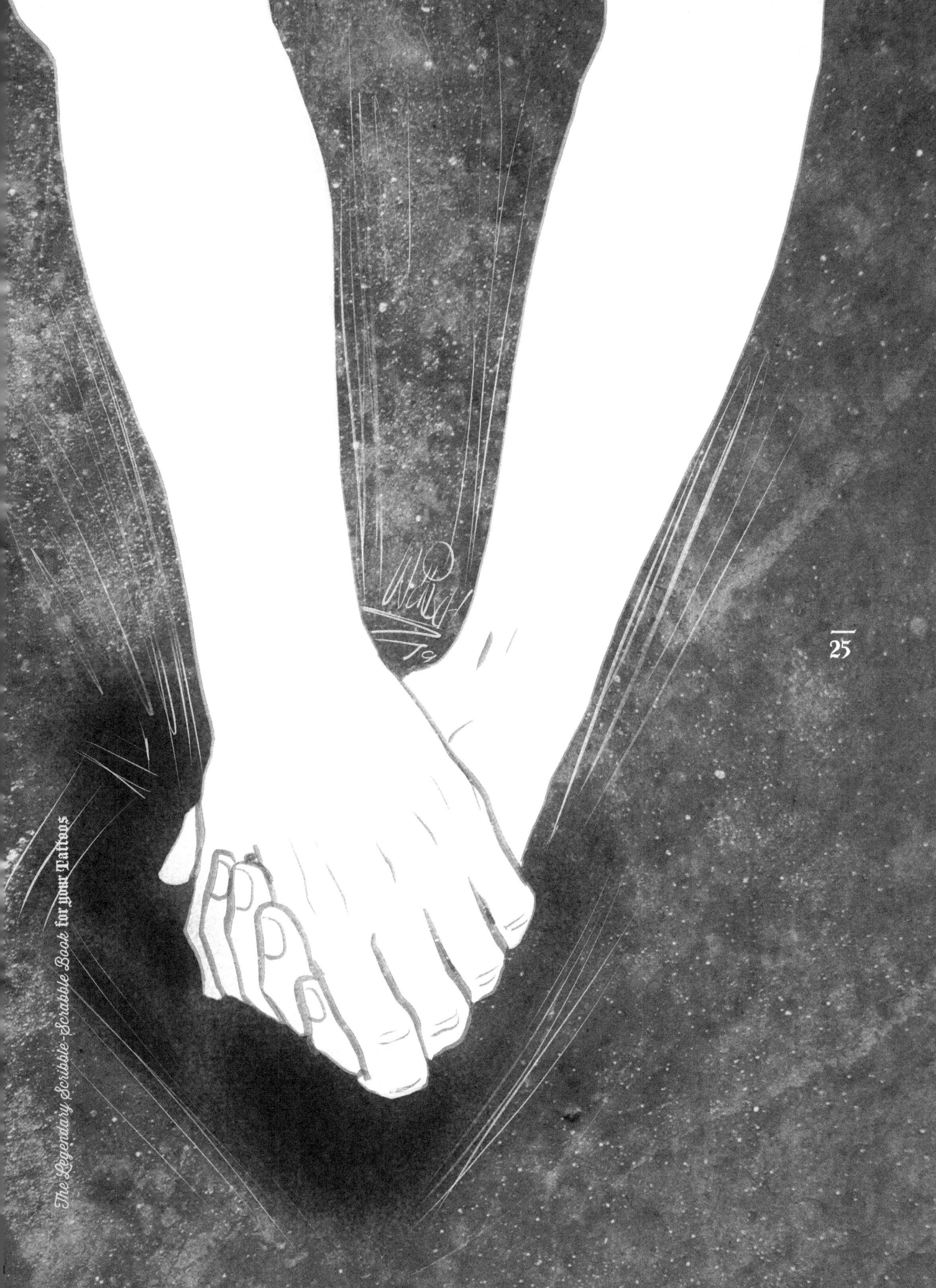

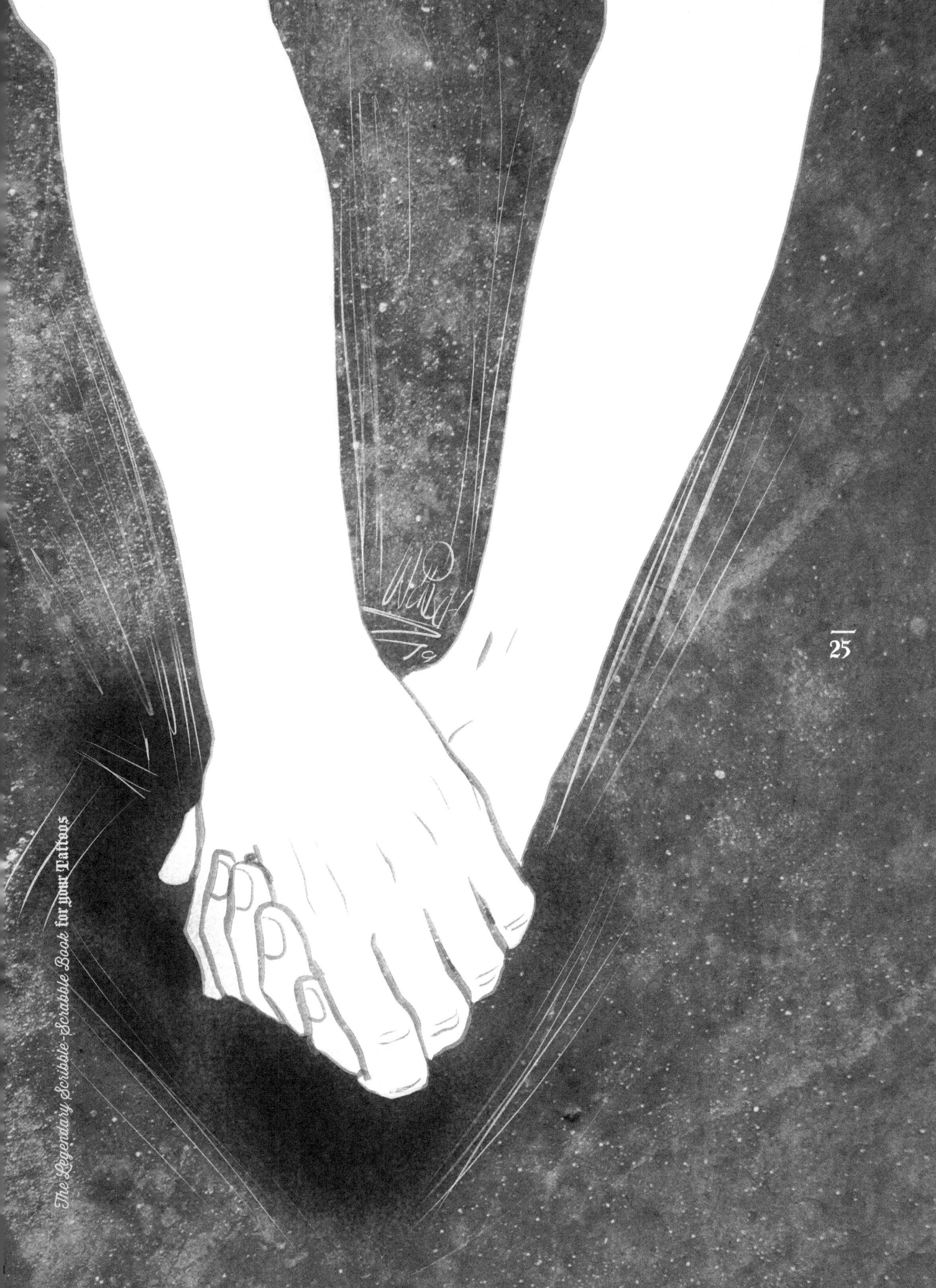The Legendary Scribble-Scrabble Book for your Tattoos

25

26

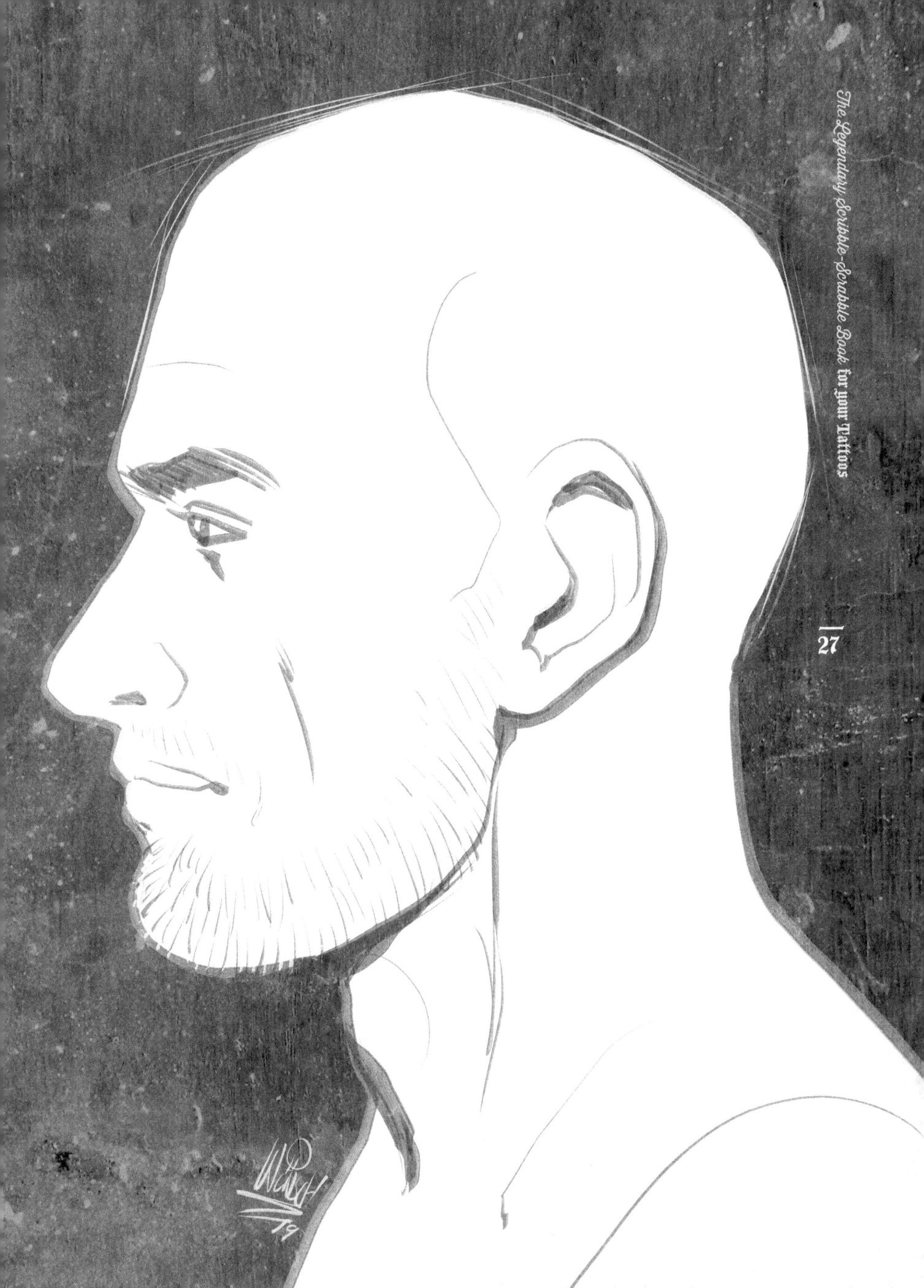

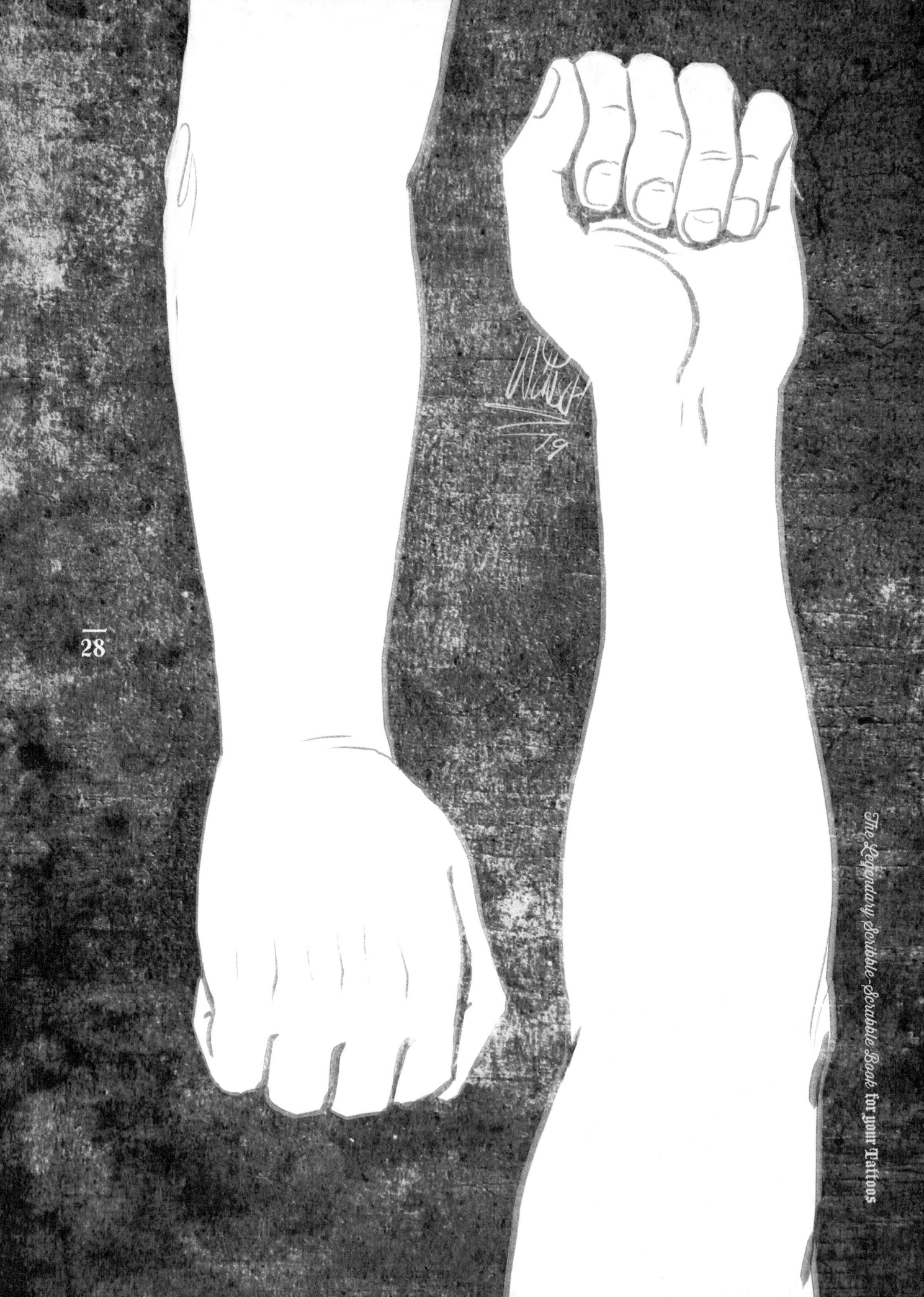

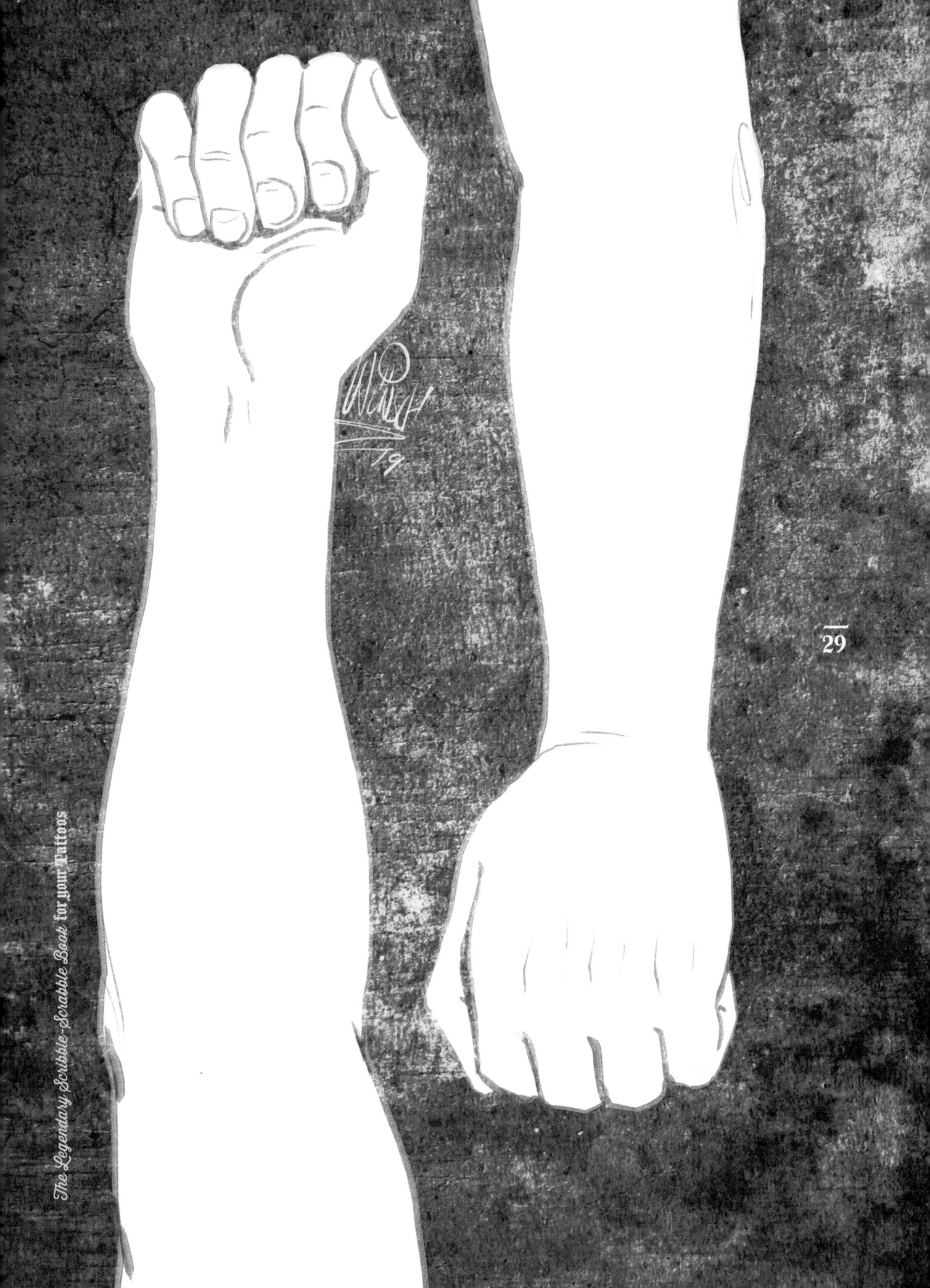

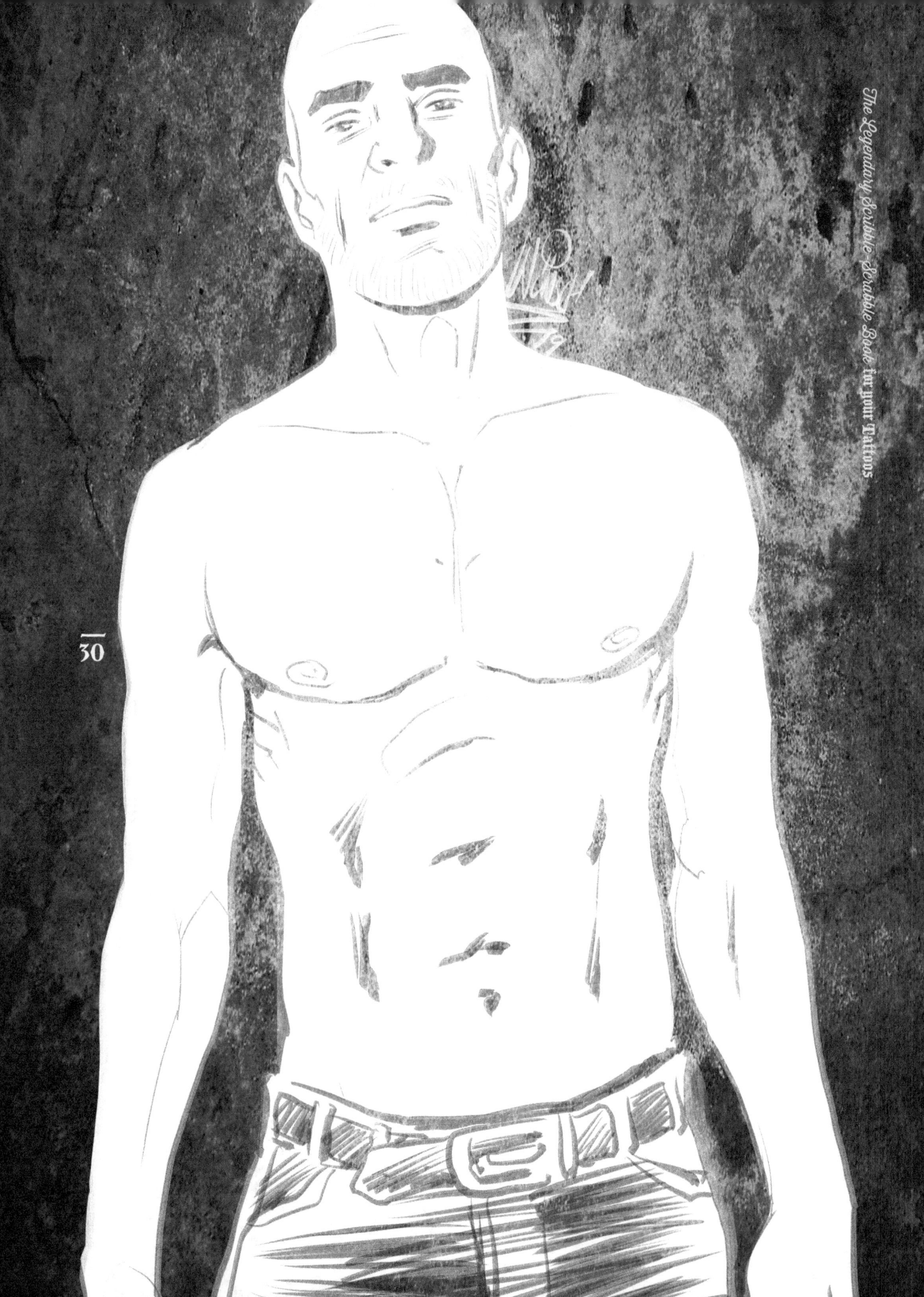

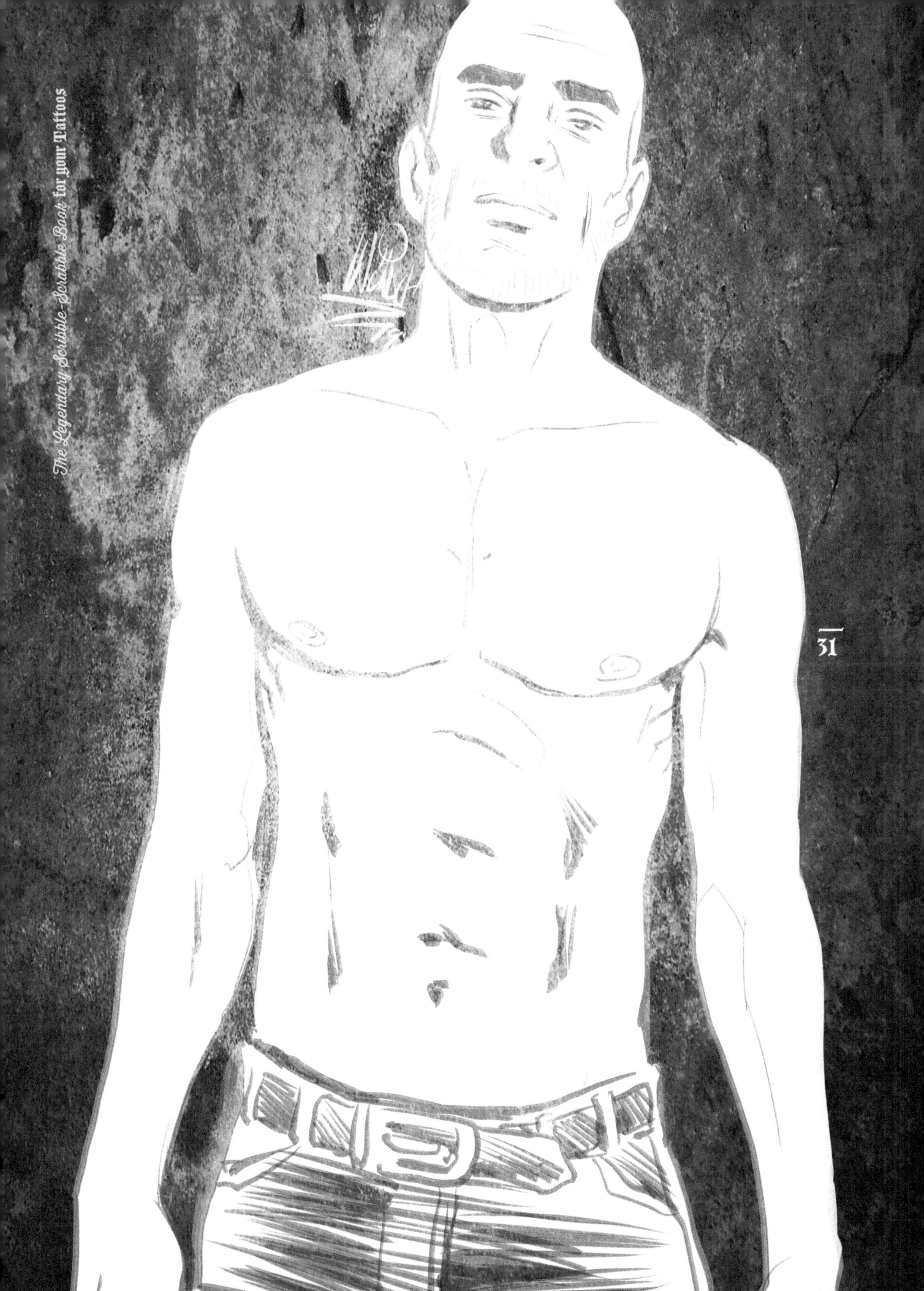

31

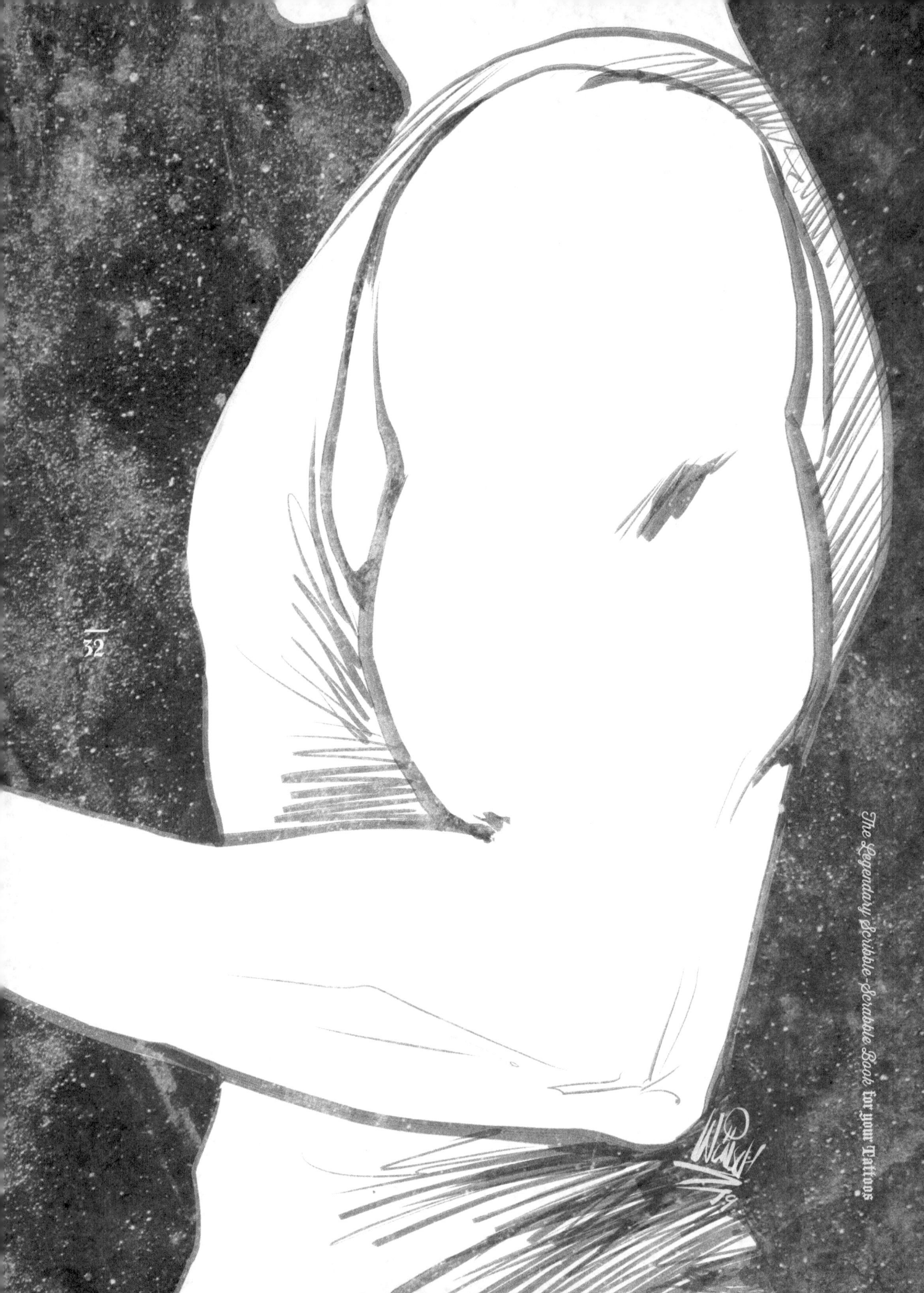

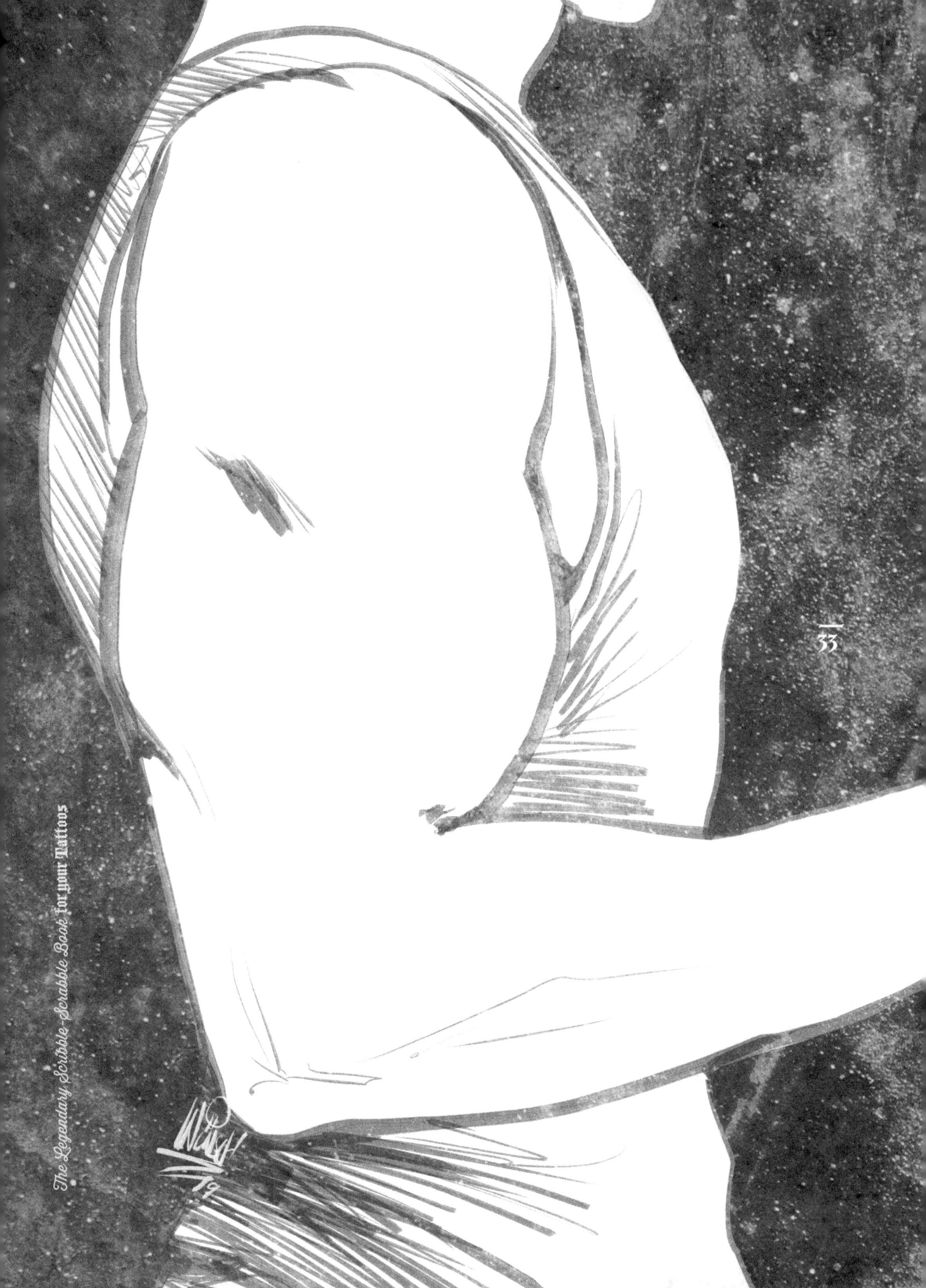

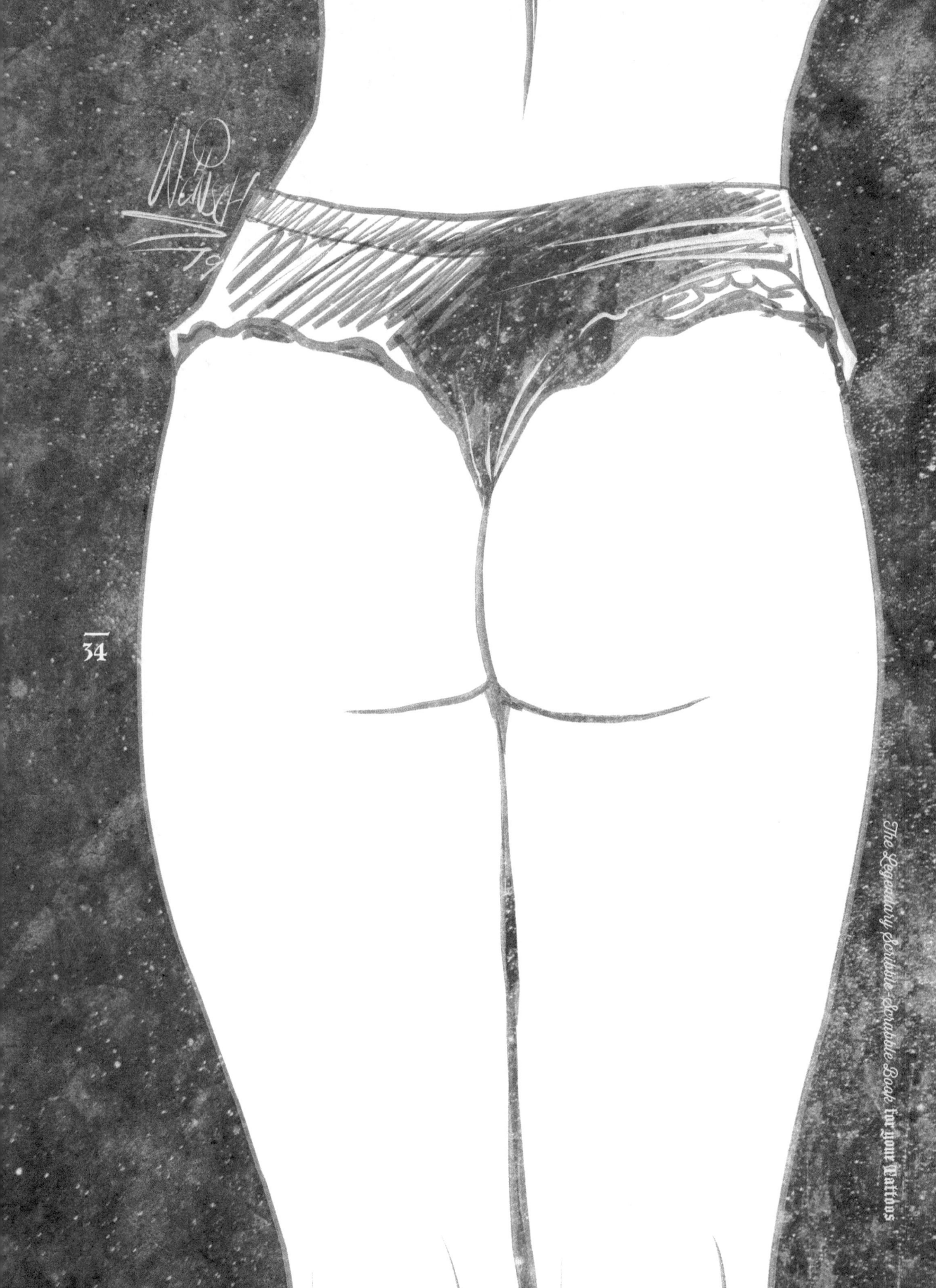

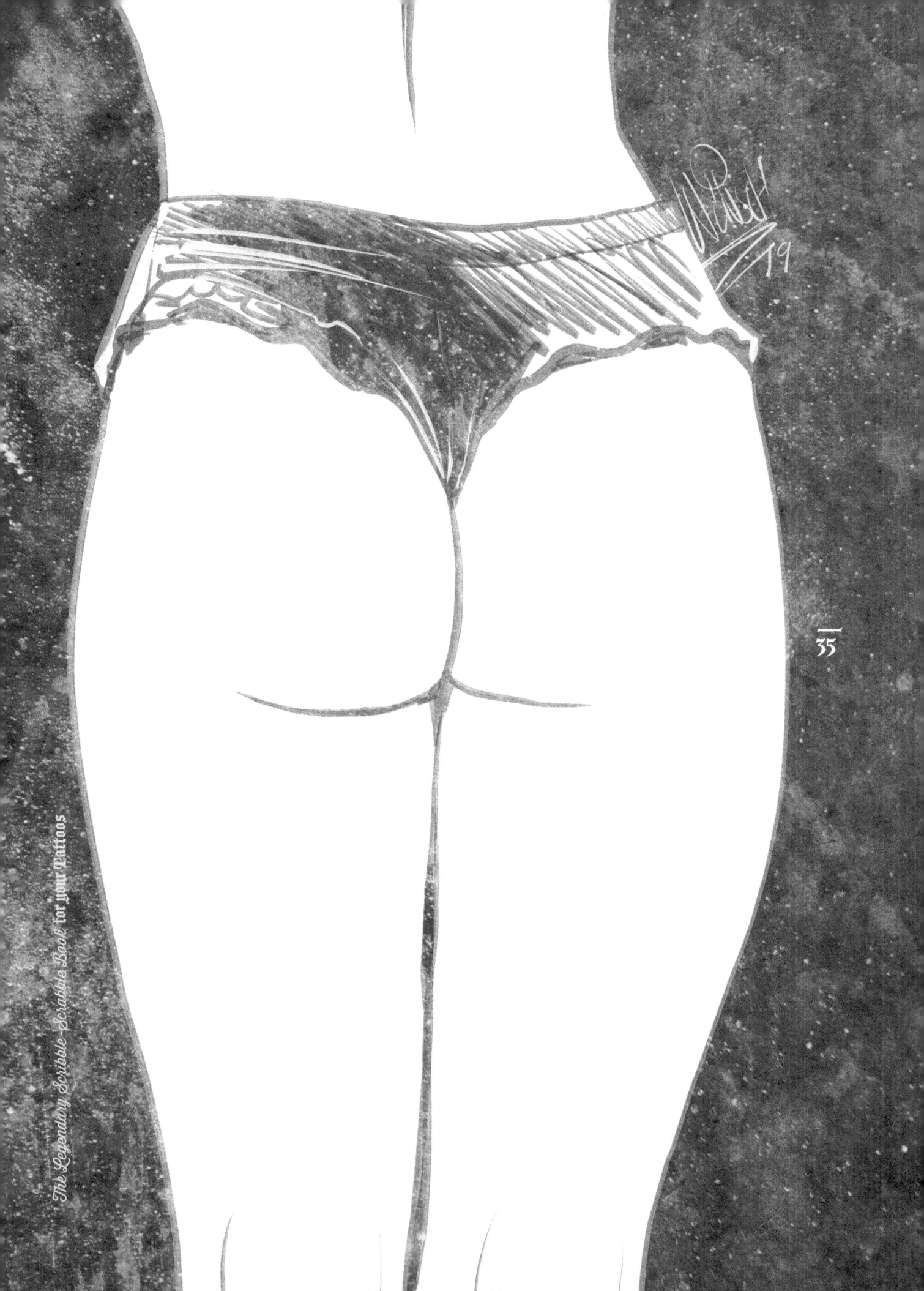

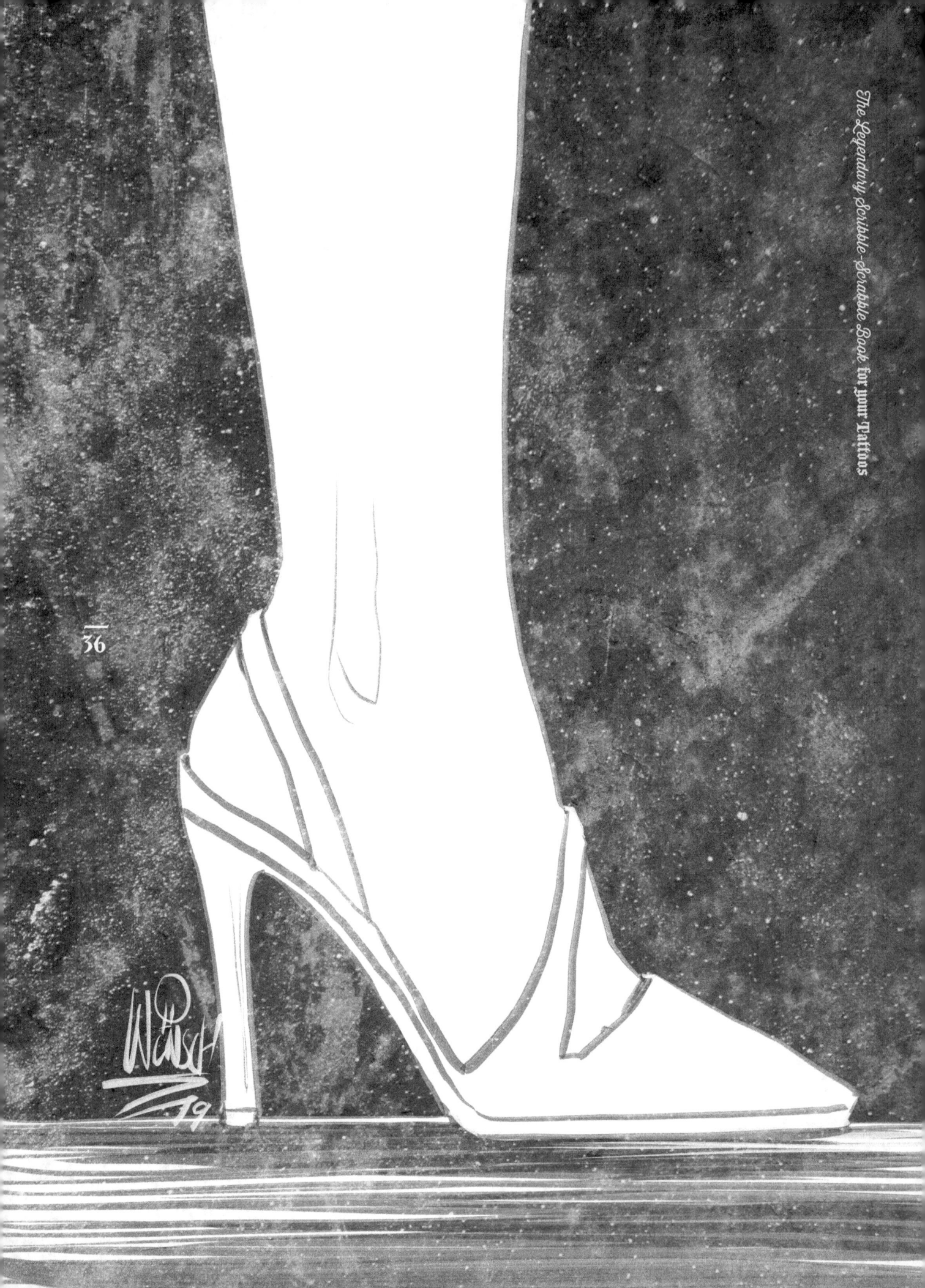

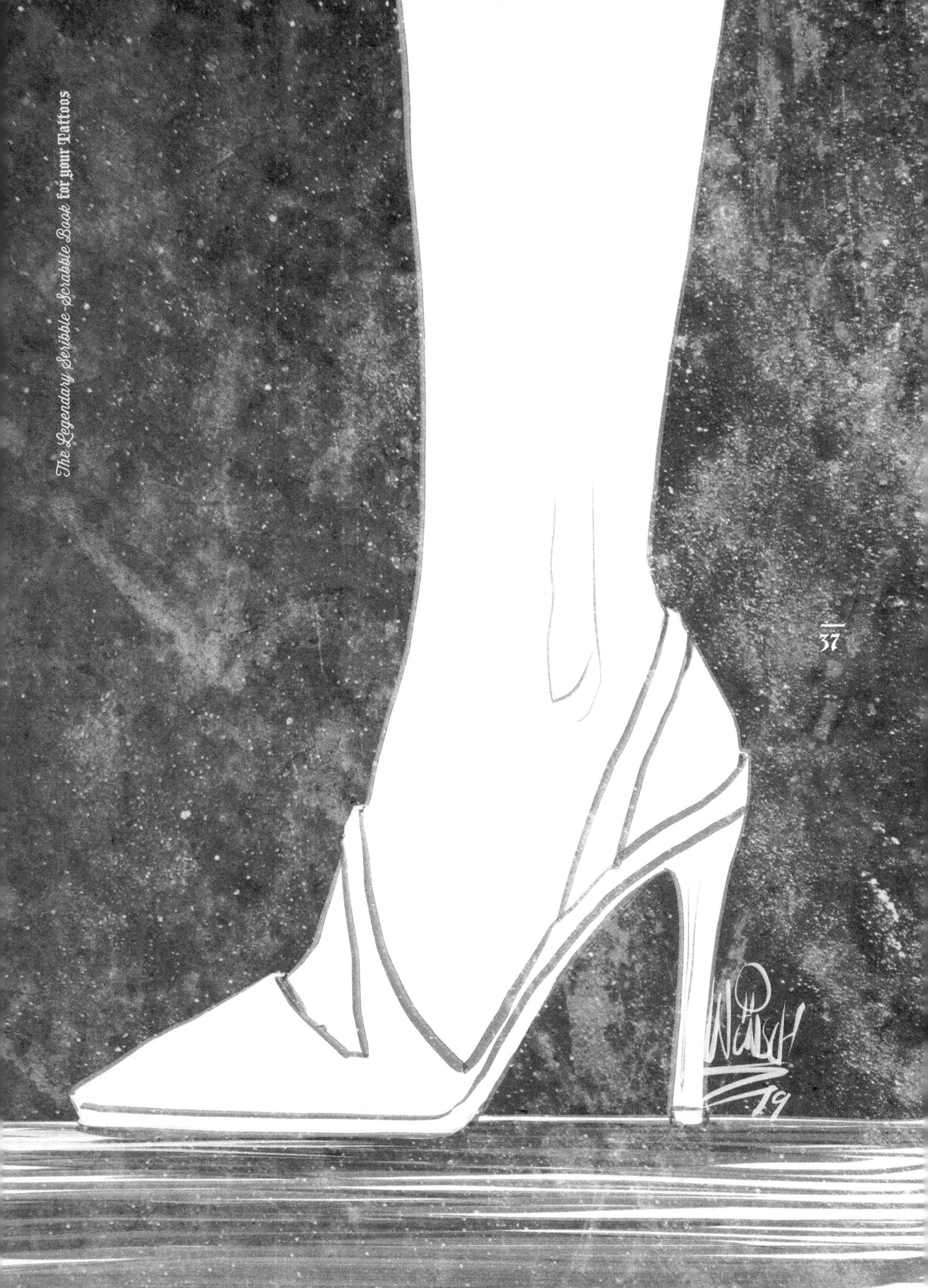

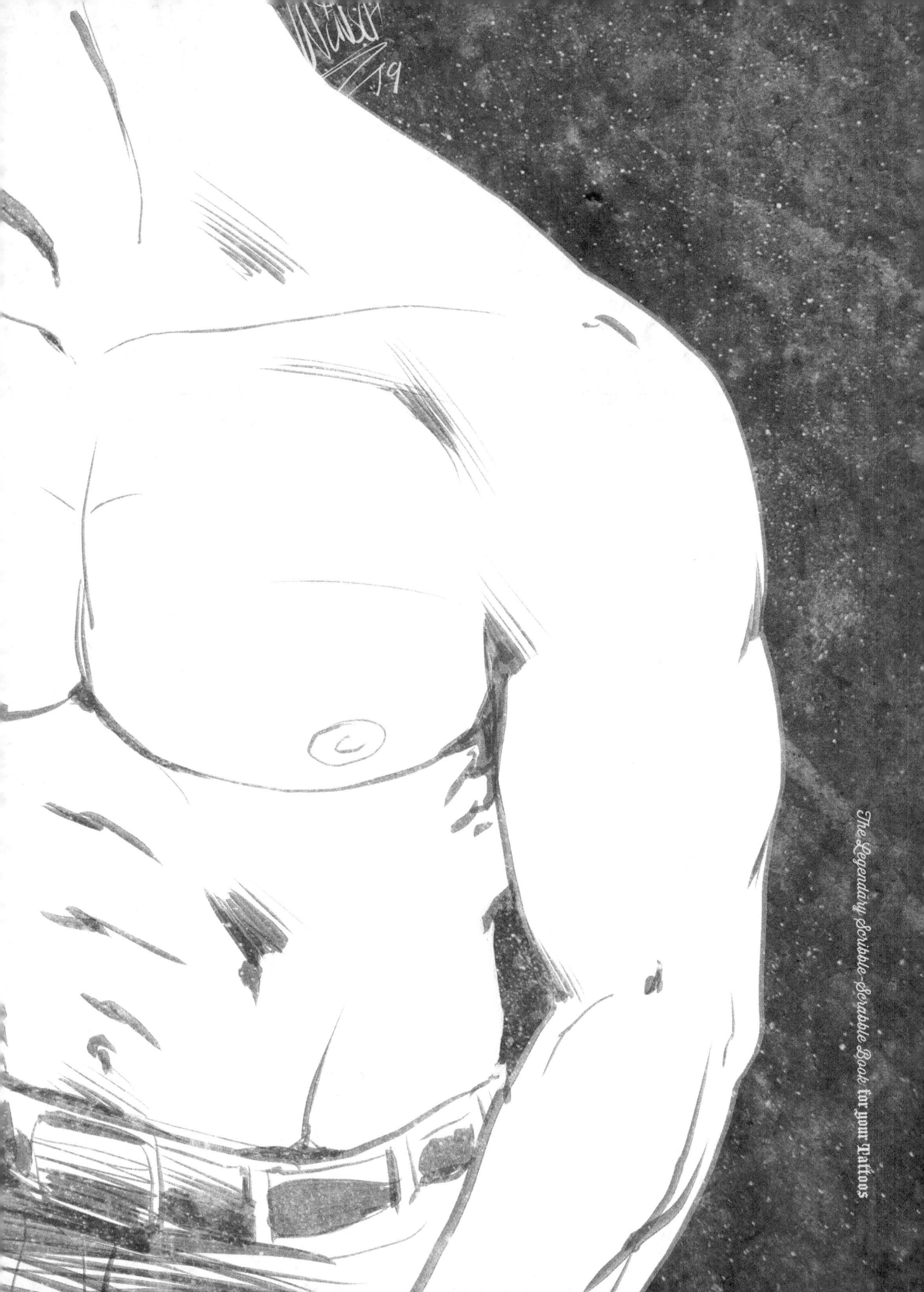

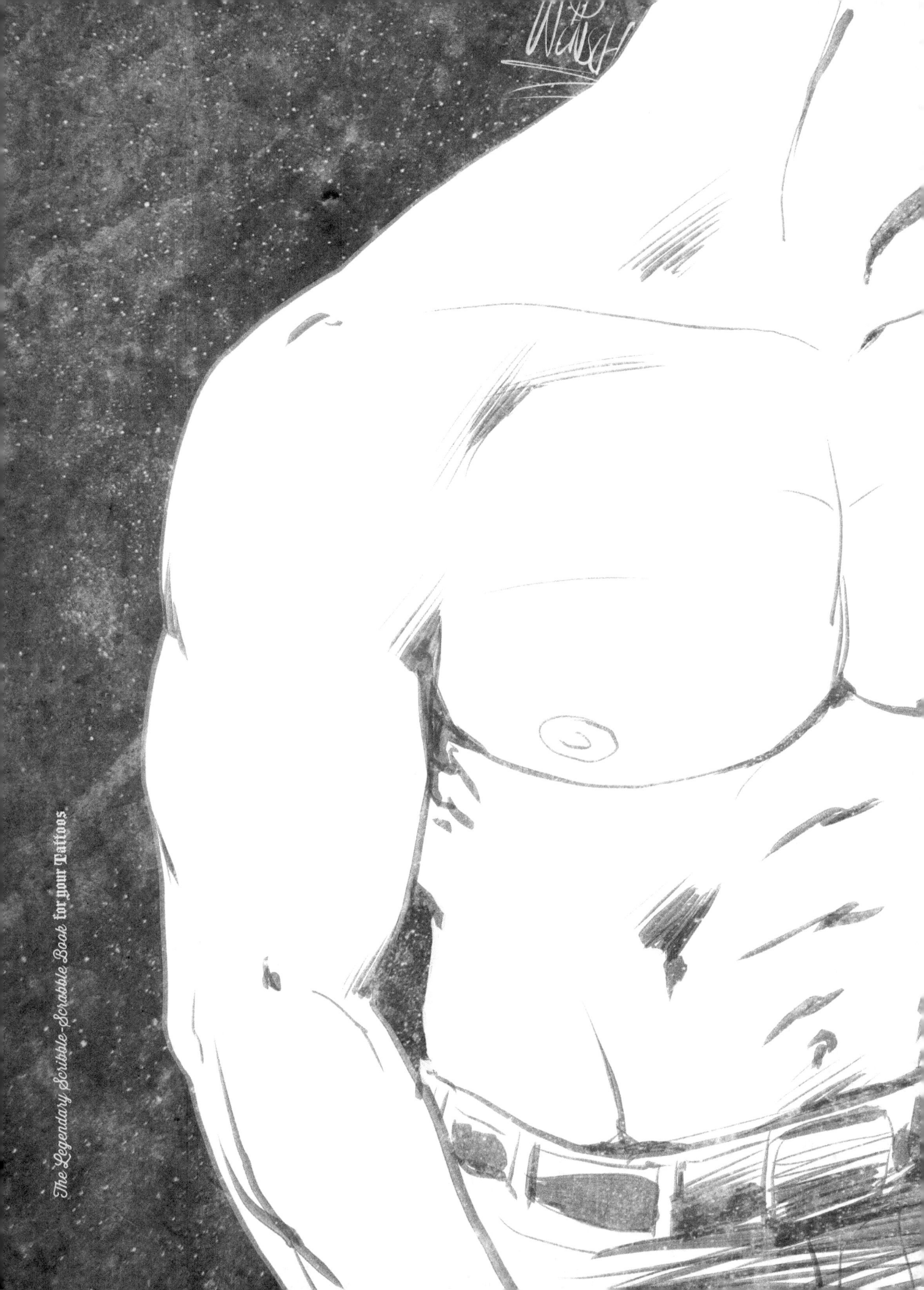

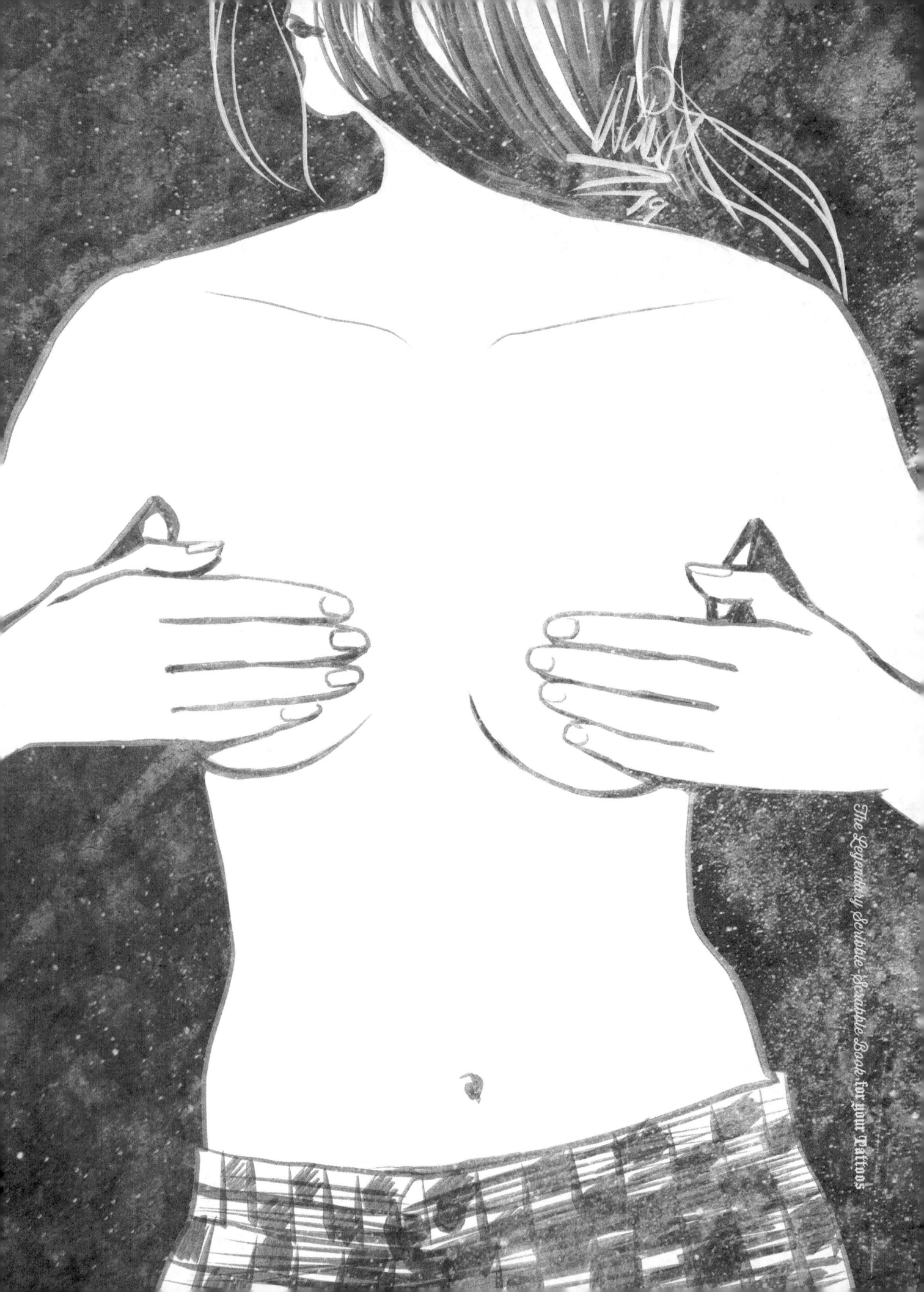

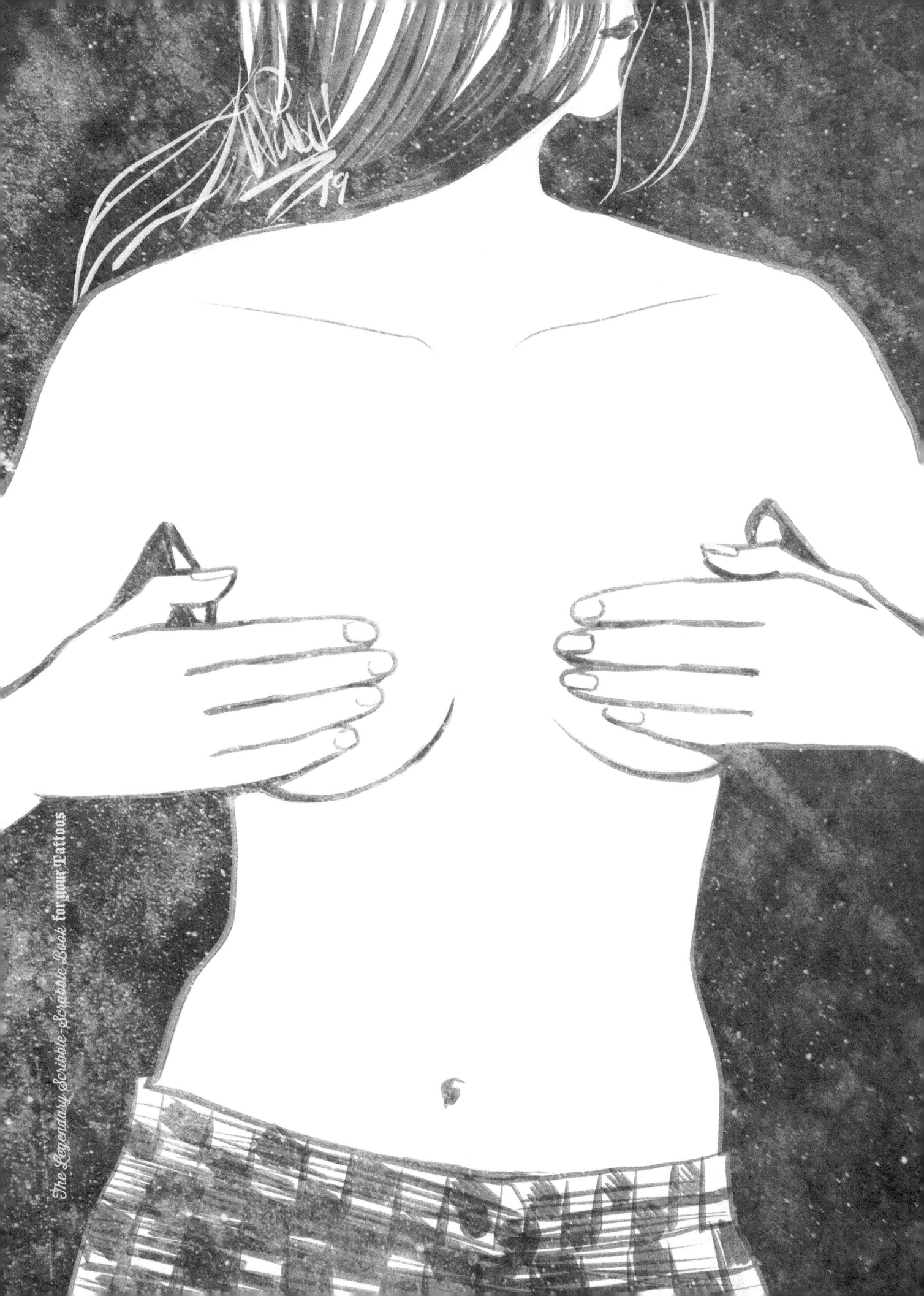

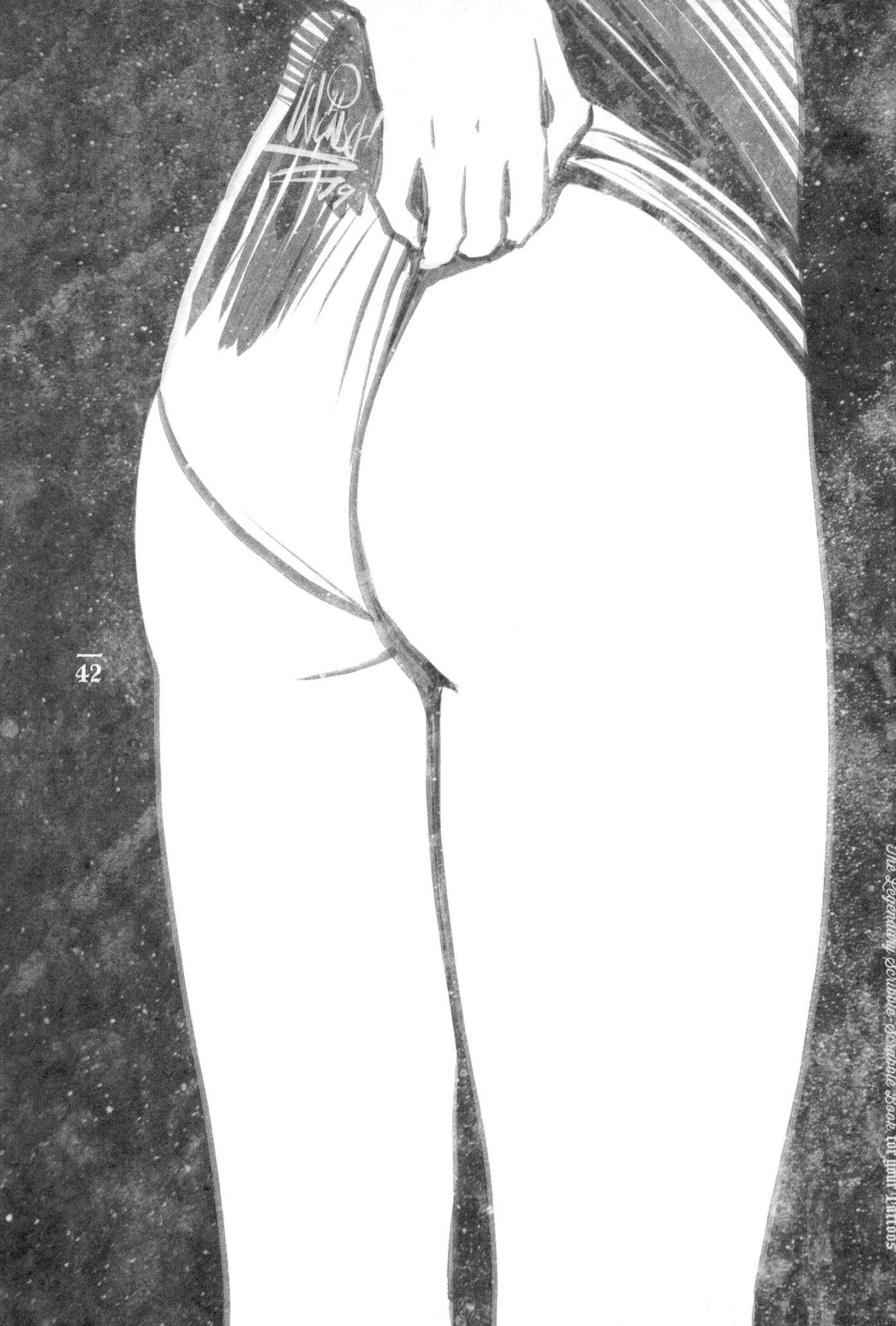

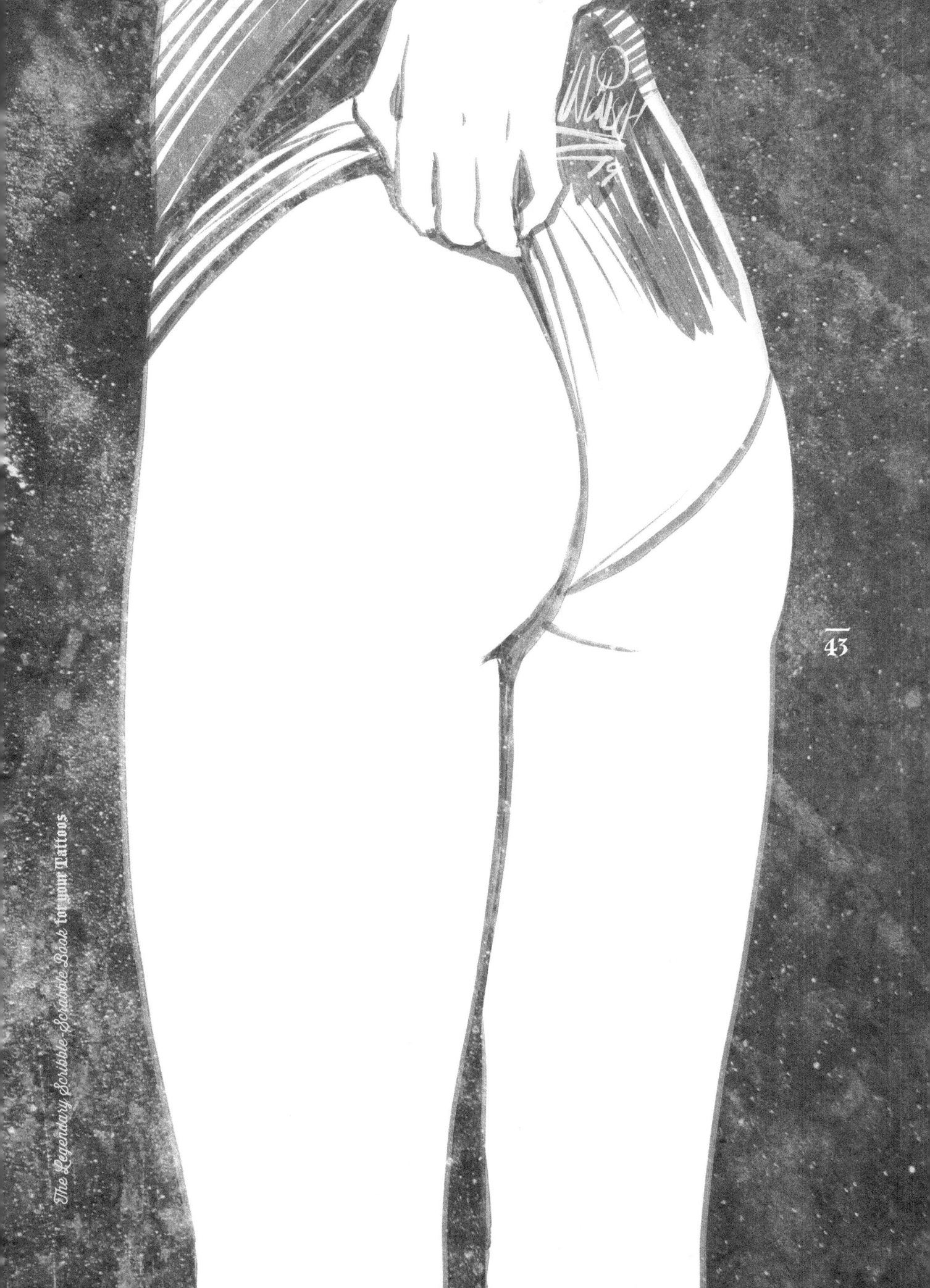

The Legendary Scribble-Scrabble Book for your Tattoos

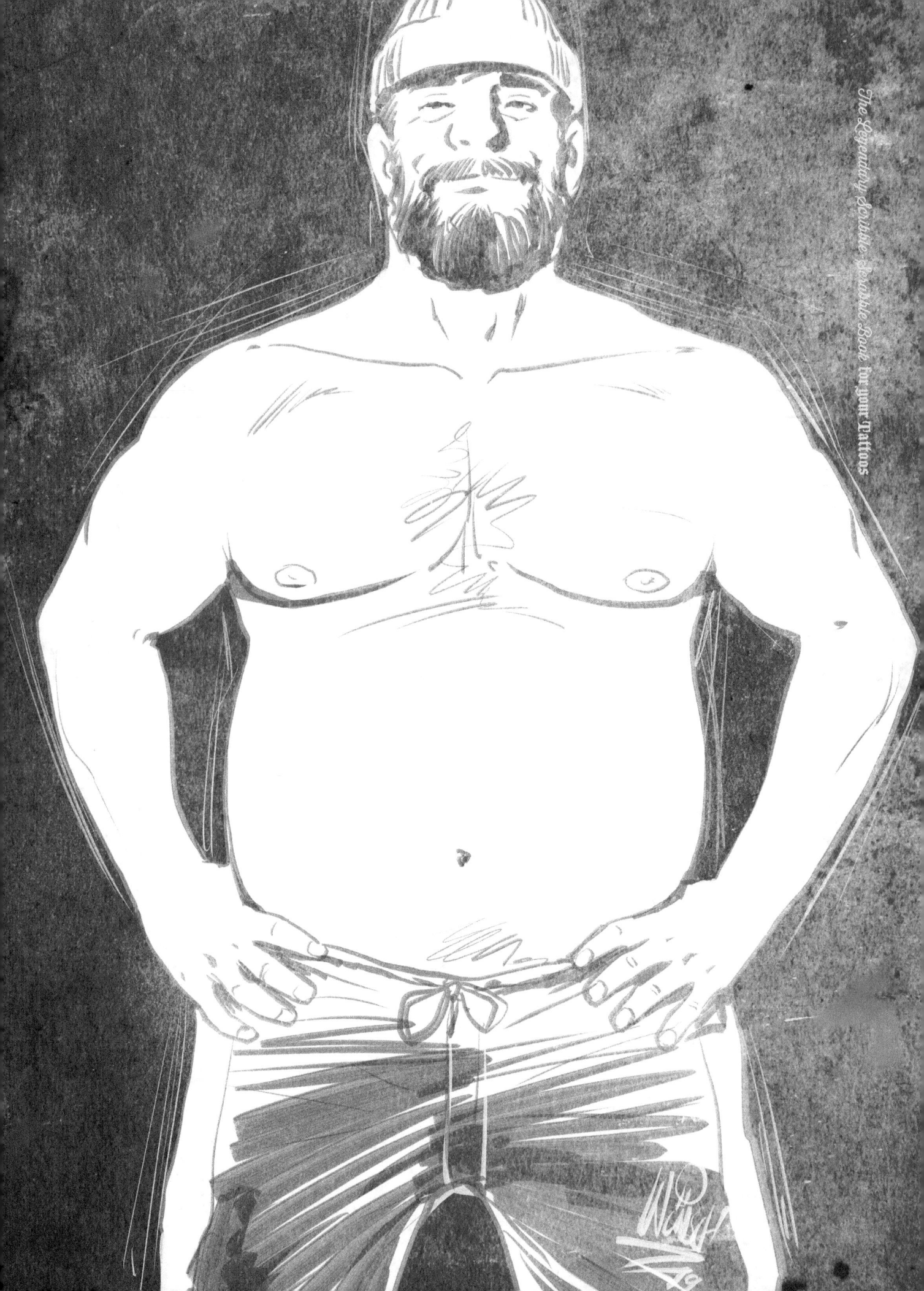

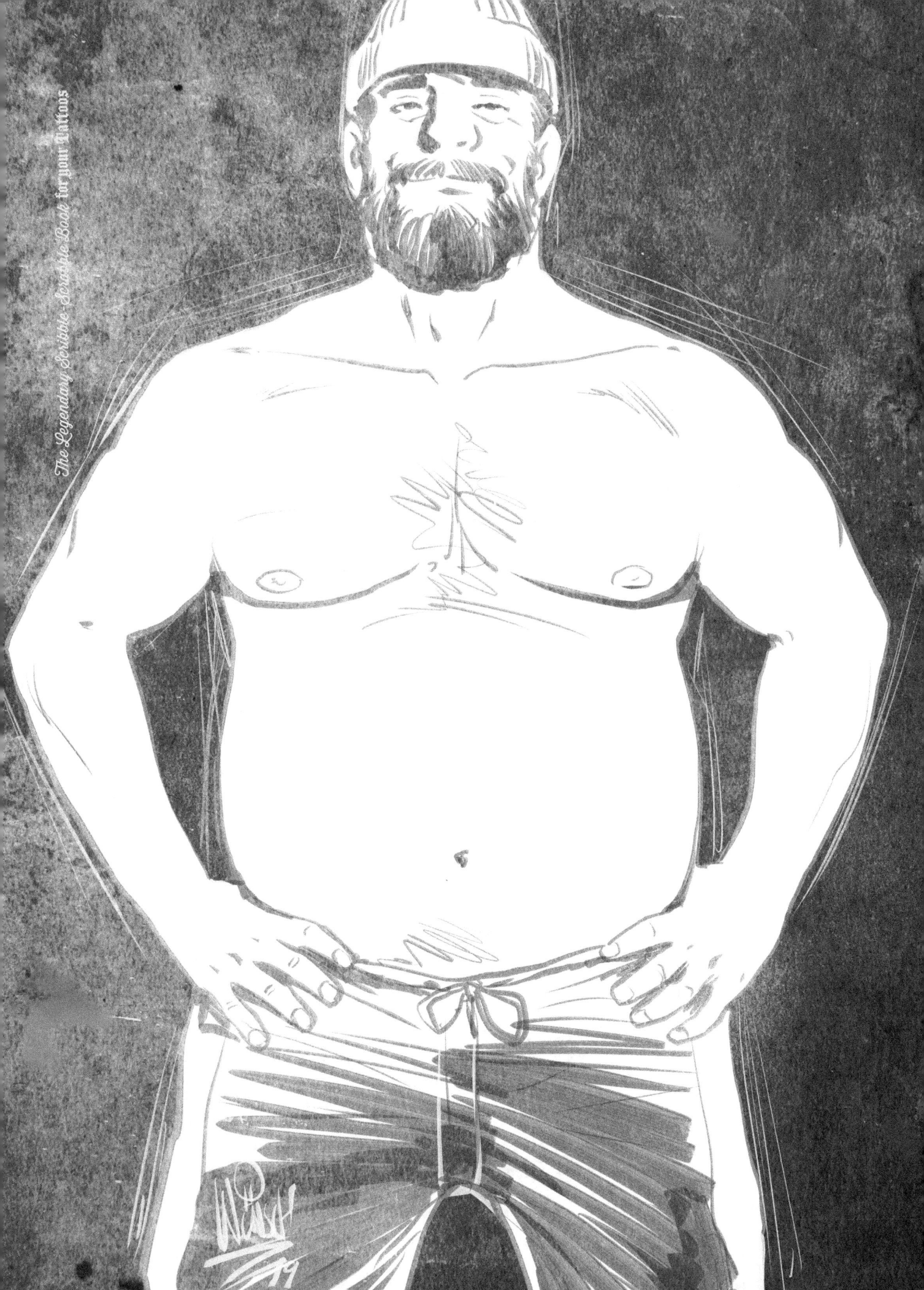

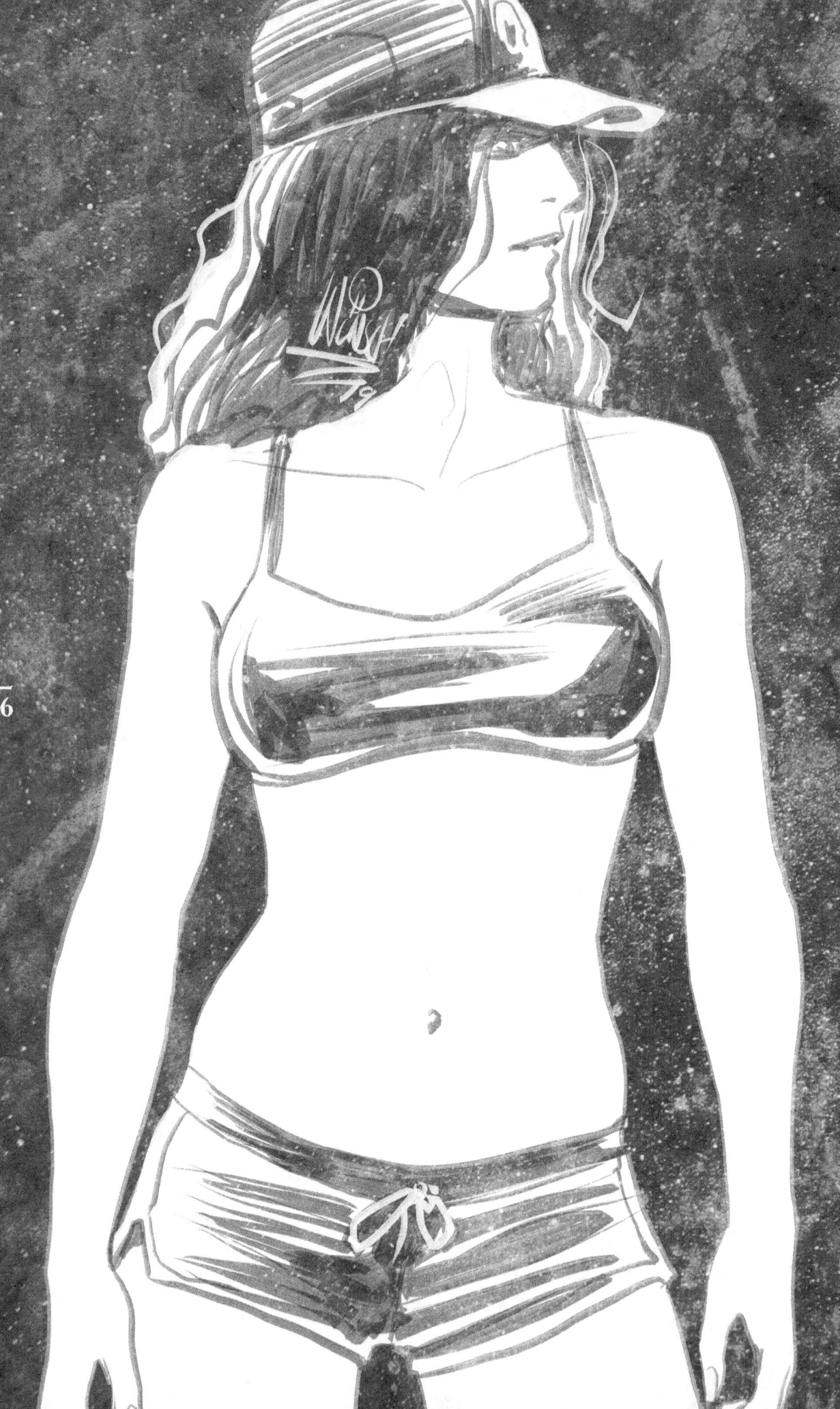

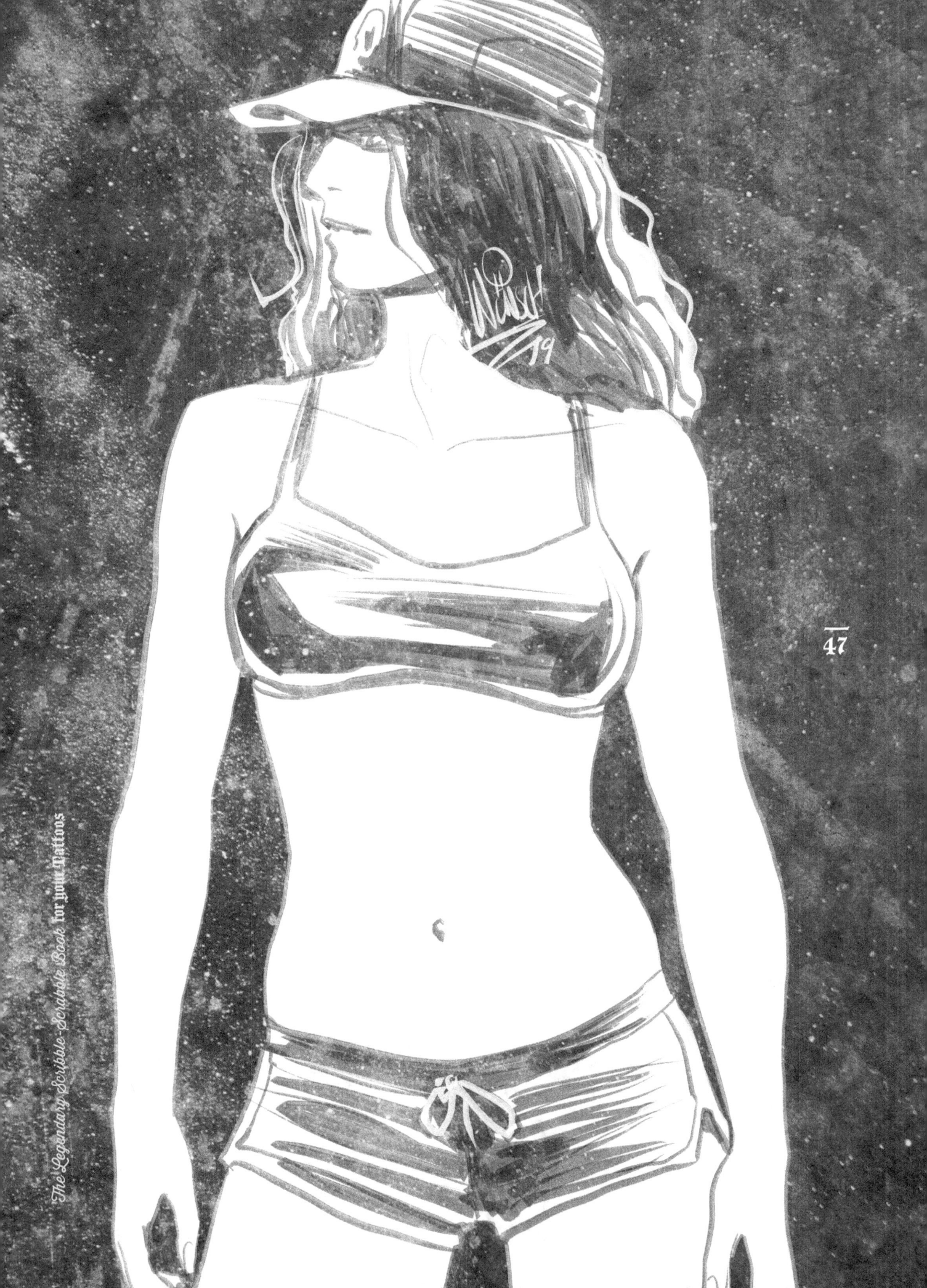

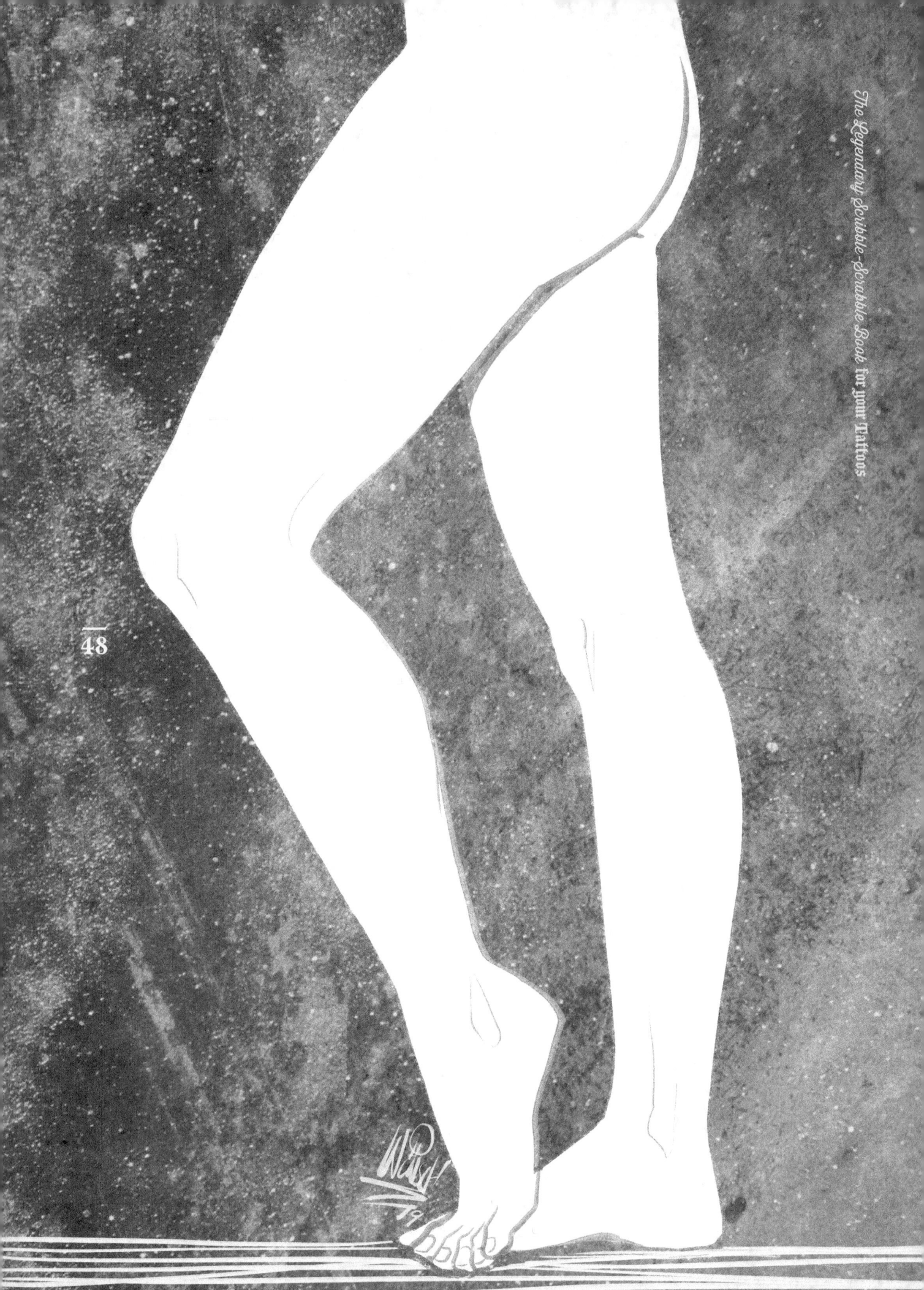

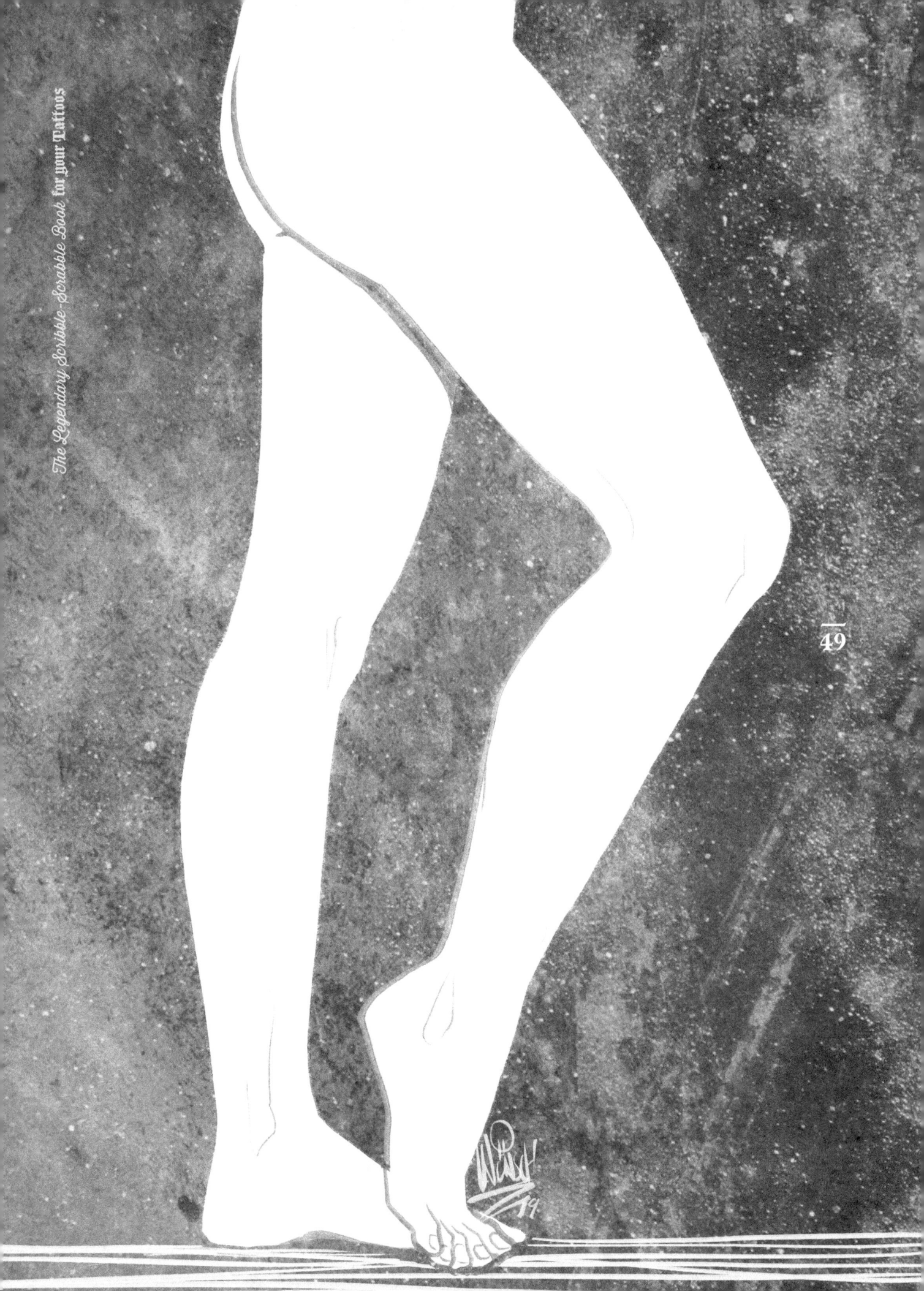

49

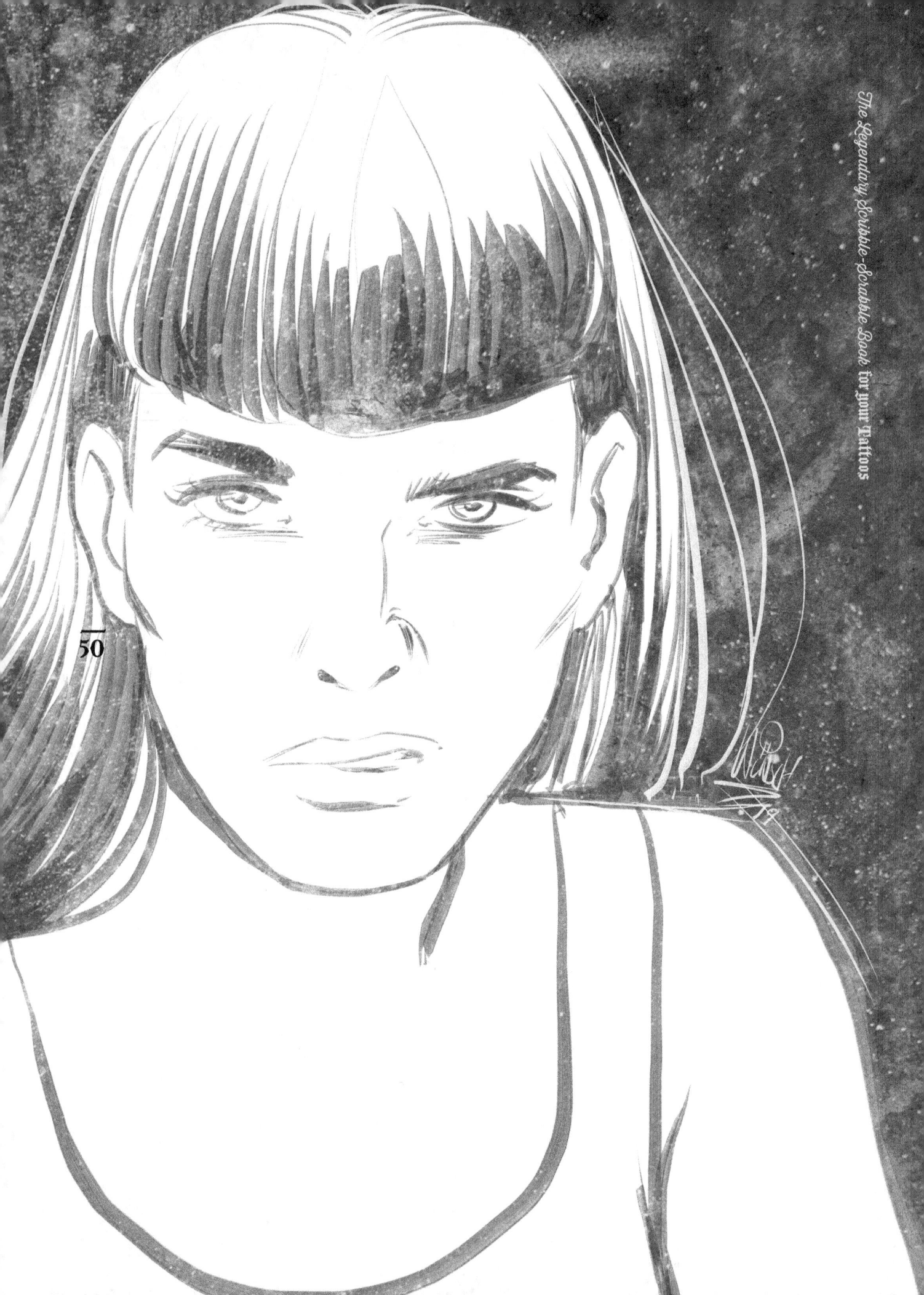

50

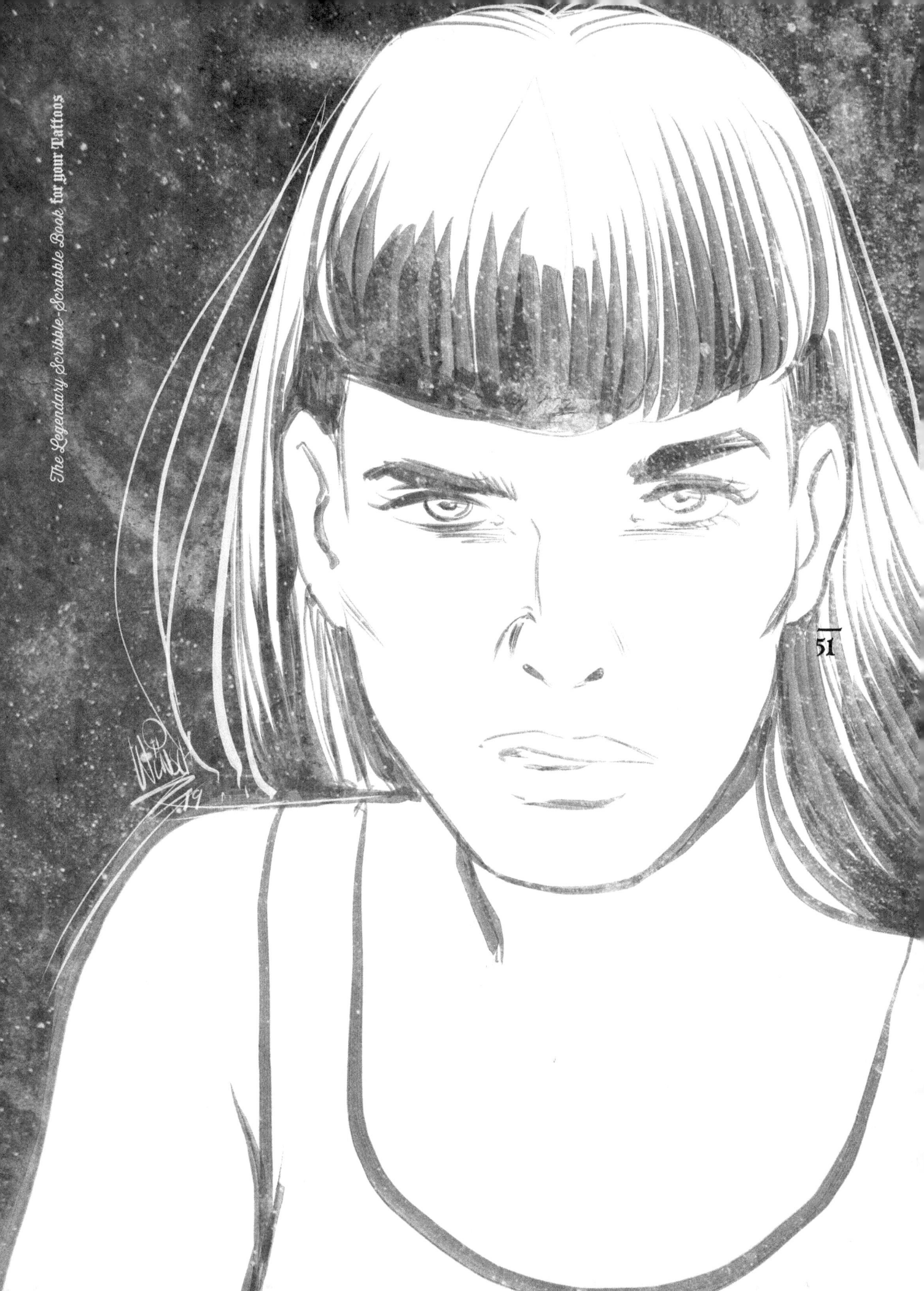

51

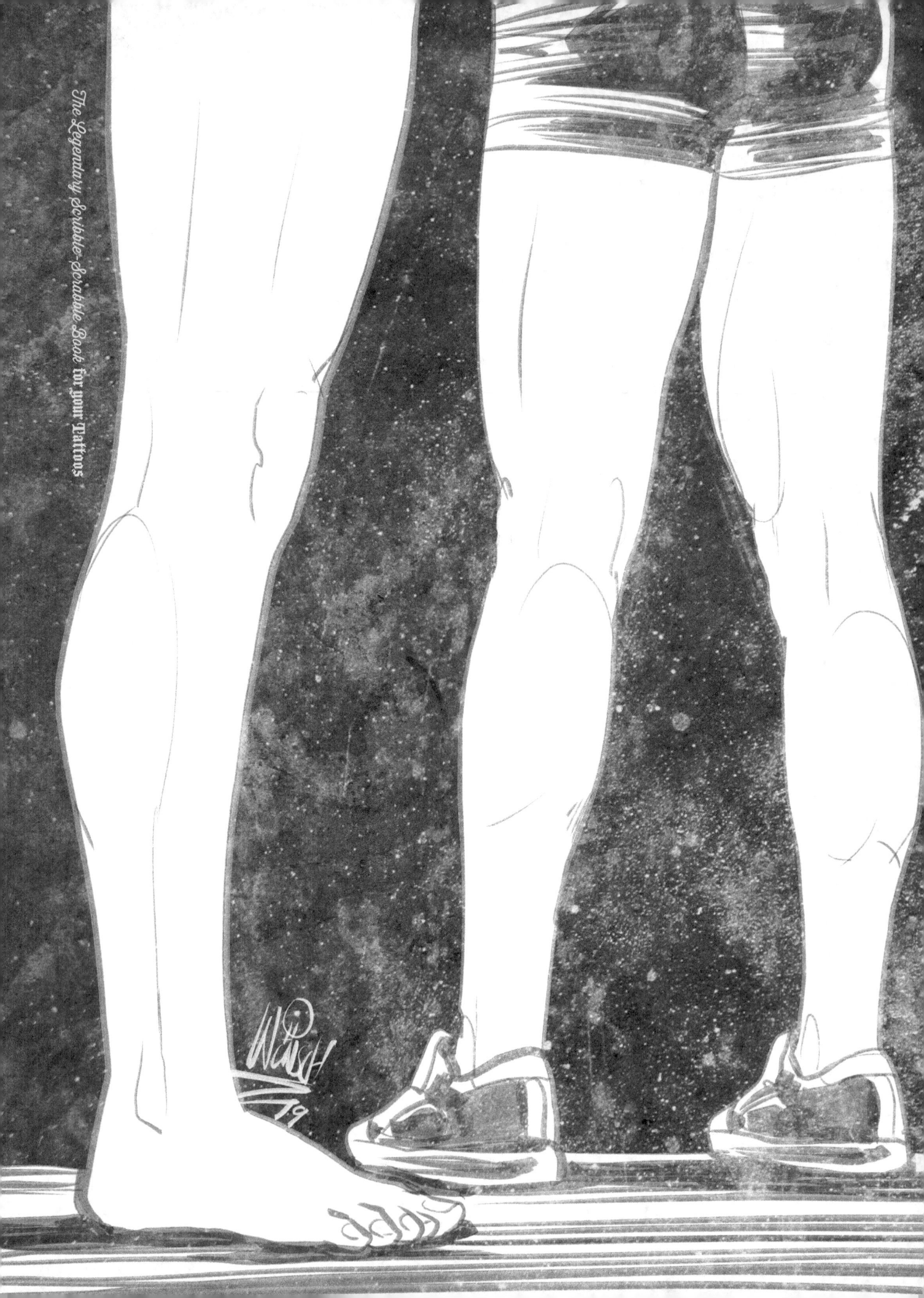

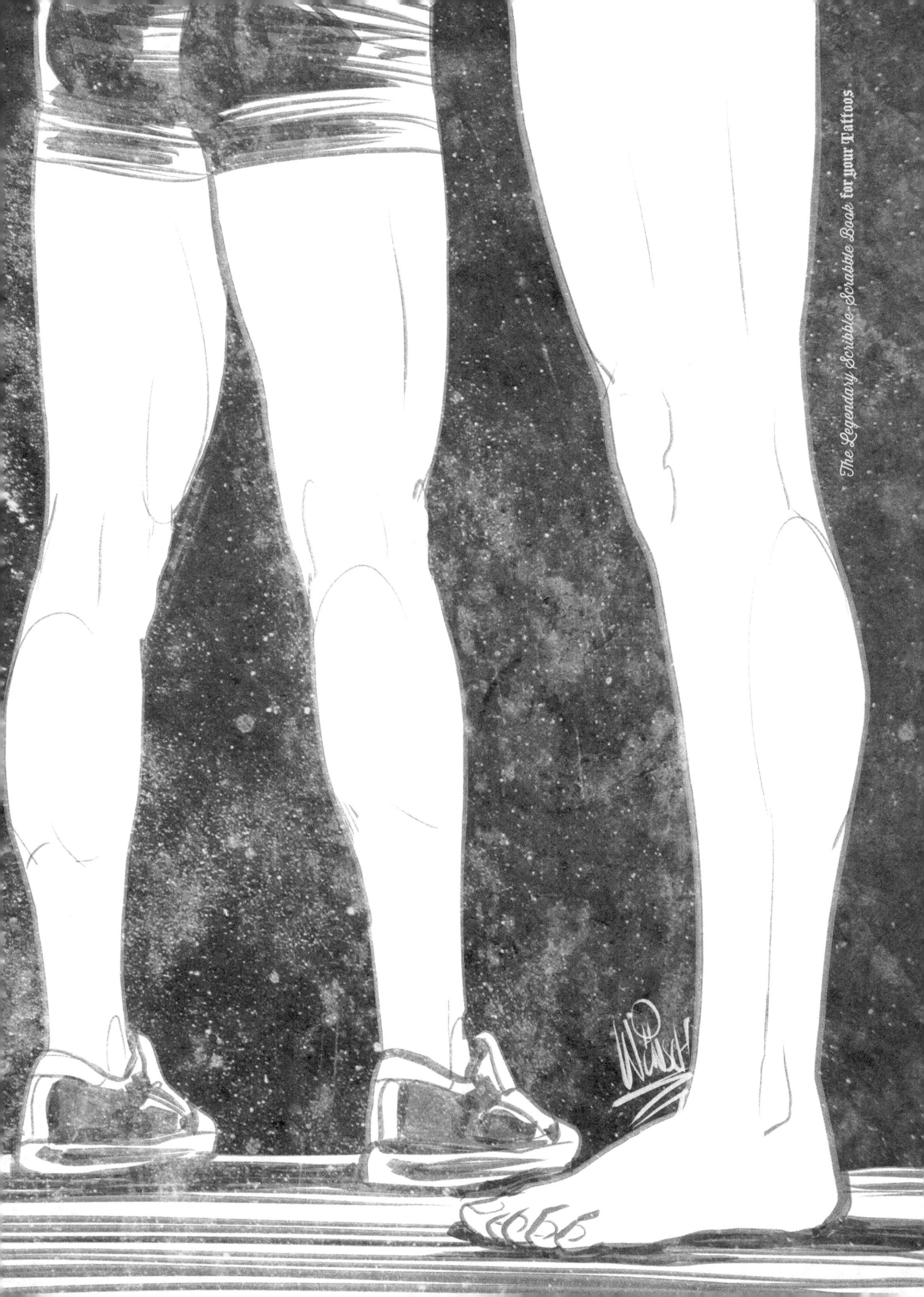

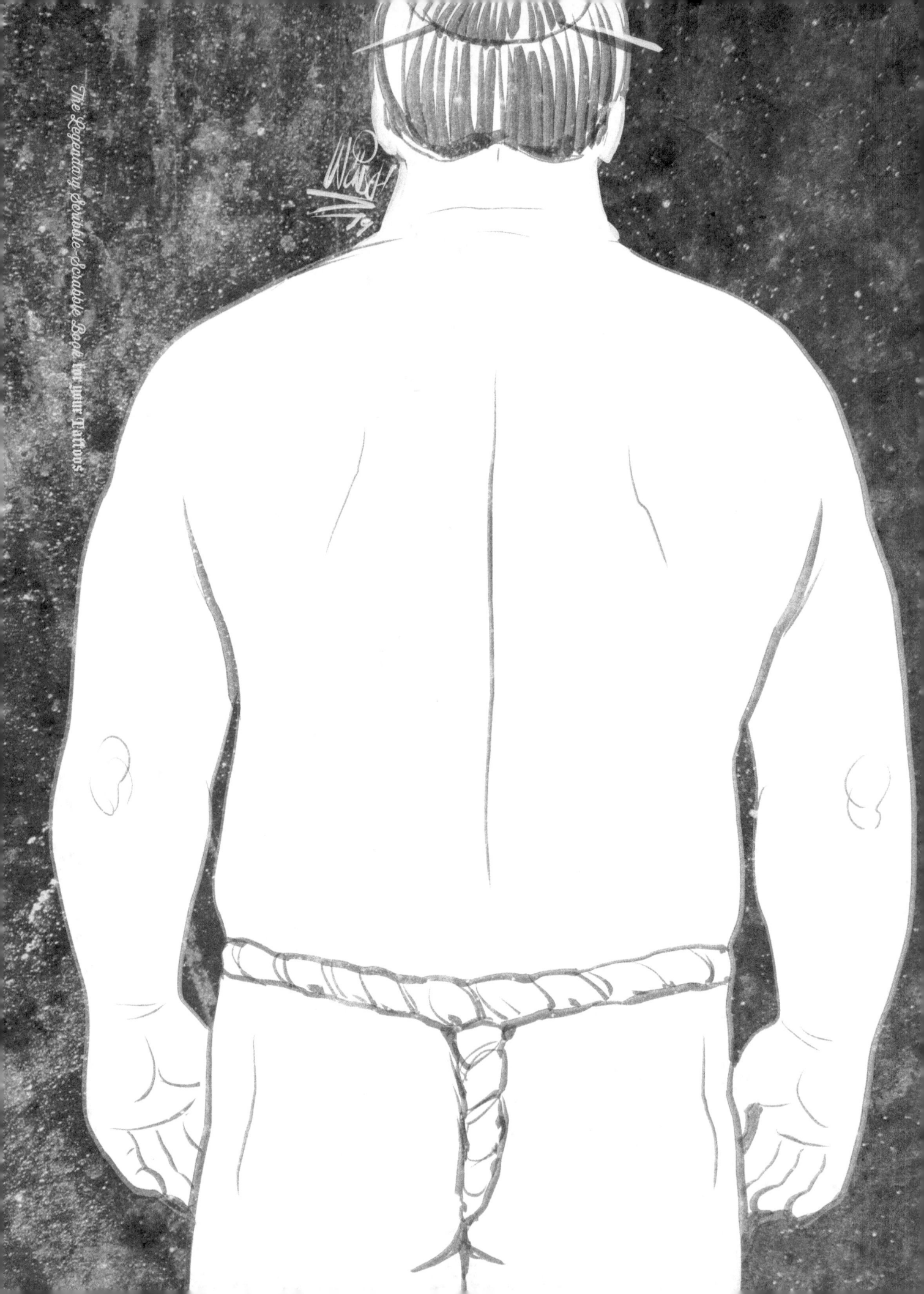

www.ingramcontent.com/pod-product-compliance
Lightning Source LLC
Chambersburg PA
CBHW081004220526
45467CB00008B/2693